ATLANTA

A FUN-FILLED, FACT-PACKED TRAVEL & ACTIVITY BOOK

by Rosanne Knorr

John Muir Publications
Santa Fe, New Mexico

Kids learn about electricity at SciTrek

John Muir Publications, P.O. Box 613, Santa Fe, NM 87504

Printed in the United States of America.
First edition. First printing February 1997

Library of Congress Cataloging-in-Publication Data.
Kidding Around Atlanta/Rosanne Knorr. — 1st ed.
p. cm.
Summary: Provides information on landmarks, museums, parks, sports, activities, entertainment, restaurants, and more things to see and do in Atlanta.
Includes index.
ISBN 1-56261-334-0 (pbk.)
1. Atlanta (Ga.)—Guidebooks—Juvenile literature. 2. Family recreation—Georgia—Atlanta—Guidebooks—Juvenile literature [1.Atlanta (Ga.)—Guides] I. Title.
F294.A83K58 1997
917.58'2310443—dc21 96-47354
CIP
AC

Editors Rob Crisell, Kristin Shahane, Lizann Flatt
Production Nikki Rooker
Graphics Joanne Jakub, Jane MacCarter
Typesetting Kathleen Sparkes, White Hart Design
Activities Rob Crisell, Bobi Martin
Cover Design Caroline Van Remortel
Illustrations Stacy Venturi-Pickett
Maps Susan Harrison
Cover Photo Governor's Mansion, Aristock Inc./Gordon Kilgore
Back Cover Photo Six Flags over Georgia
Printer Burton & Mayer

Distributed to the book trade by
Publishers Group West
Emeryville, California

CONTENTS

COLOR THE ROUTE FROM YOUR HOMETOWN TO ATLANTA

If you're flying, color the states you'll fly over. If you're driving, color the states you'll drive through. If you live in Georgia, color the states you have traveled to.

WELCOME TO ATLANTA!

Lake Lanier

ATLANTA IS A CITY OF OPPOSITES. IT HAS A LONG and fascinating history, but its modern buildings make it look brand new. It's a thriving business center, but Atlanta is known for its beautiful trees and mild climate. It's the center of the Southeastern United States, but it attracts visitors and businesses from around the world.

With all this variety, Atlanta is a wonderful place to live and an interesting place to visit. We're happy to have you here . . . and we hope you discover many things to enjoy in Atlanta as you learn more about it!

How to Use This Book

You can use this book any way you want. There are no rules. Read it yourself, or share it with your parents to decide together what your family will do.

You can start on page one and read the book all the way through to the end. Or you can skip around and pick the subjects you're interested in. If you want to see animals, look through Chapter 3. If you're in an active mood, you might want to check out the parks in Chapter 2 for places to hike or fly a kite. However you choose to use this book, enjoy!

The First Settlers

Centuries before the city of Atlanta was founded, the forest that covered this area was home to native American Indians. This wilderness was a good place to live because the land was filled with lush vegetation, fish, and wildlife. The Cherokee Indians lived in the area that's now called Atlanta.

In 1837, a town was founded here. It was named Terminus, meaning the end. The name was appropriate because the town was the southern end of a railroad line. The small town of Terminus was later named Marthasville. In 1845, the city was named Atlanta, a word that was made up to be the feminine version of "Atlantic."

Atlanta is lush with lakes and greenery.

HINTS ON ATLANTA TRAVEL

Kids can be comfortable in Atlanta. The city tends to be a casual place, so you can wear jeans or shorts almost anywhere. Of course, you might want to dress up a little if your parents take you to a special place or event.

In summer, Atlanta gets very hot and humid, so bring lots of shorts and tops, and don't forget a bathing suit. Winter is usually mild, but occasionally it can get very cold. You probably won't need boots because Atlanta rarely gets snow, but bring a warm jacket if you'll be here in December, January, or February. In spring or fall, a sweater or light jacket will be enough.

Here are some ideas of what to take with you when you're out exploring Atlanta!

The Civil War

Due to its central location, Atlanta became a prime target for the Union Army during the country's Civil War. Confederate troops fought together to defend the city, but they had too few troops and supplies. Union troops under General William T. Sherman marched into the city on September 2, 1864, after a 117-day attack and ordered all civilians to leave. The Confederates torched their own supplies in order to keep the Union army from getting them. Later, Sherman's Union army set fire to what remained of the city in his destructive "March to the Sea" through Georgia.

The wreckage was complete; the city was in ashes. But Atlanta's people were brave and determined to rebuild an even greater city. It was this spirit that later captured the world's imagination through the famous novel by Margaret Mitchell, *Gone with the Wind*.

It wasn't long before Atlanta rebounded. It was the headquarters for the government in charge of reconstructing the Union after the war, and once more Atlanta became the financial, governmental, industrial, transportation, and retail hub of the Southeast. In 1895, the city proved it was finally back on its feet by throwing a huge party called the Cotton States and International Exposition.

Plaque describing the Surrender of Atlanta

Atlanta on the Rise

Atlanta's positive spirit helped it grow and thrive. Atlantans worked together to improve the city, and soon it became known as one of the most advanced cities in the South. During the 1960s, there were many riots across the United States, when opinion in some American cities was divided over the issue of treating blacks and whites as equals. But Atlanta made history for peacefully uniting blacks and whites by providing equal opportunities for all.

Inside a Delta jet at Heritage Row

International Atlanta

Today, Atlanta is still a major hub for the South. The metropolitan area is 5,147 square miles and holds over 2.9 million people. Airplanes transport passengers from Atlanta Hartsfield International Airport to over 180 international cities. The city hosts over 45 officials from foreign countries and a growing international community. More than 2,500 international companies have their headquarters here, including several that you've probably heard of: Coca-Cola, Delta Airlines, United Parcel Service, and Holiday Inn Worldwide.

Atlanta's most recent achievement was hosting the world at the Centennial Olympic Games.

Another Beautiful Day in Paradise

Atlanta bursts with blooms each spring.

Atlanta is blessed with a beautiful location in the foothills of the Appalachian Mountains. The city is 1,050 feet above sea level, which makes it the second highest major city in the U.S. after Denver, Colorado. The city is very scenic, with gently rolling hills and flowering trees. In the spring, it's so pretty here you'll sometimes hear the radio announcer joking that it's just "another beautiful day in paradise."

From a plane, Atlanta looks like an island in a green sea. The loblolly pines are tall evergreen trees that tower overhead. In spring, dogwood trees bloom with white or pink blossoms shaped like puppy paws, and the azaleas add bright red, pink, purple, orange, and white to the scenery.

You'll also see something called kudzu along many roads. This is a green vine with large leaves. It was originally brought from Japan in the 1930s to keep dirt from eroding off steep hills, but kudzu likes Atlanta's mild climate a little too well; now it's taken over. Kudzu sometimes grows a foot a day, covering anything in its path—people joke about not standing still near it!

Atlanta's symbol is the Phoenix, the mythological bird that, like the city, rose from the ashes.

WHAT DOESN'T BELONG?

This is a scene that might have existed in Atlanta 150 years ago. But you'll notice many things that didn't exist back then. When you find something that doesn't belong, circle it. Then color in the scene. Hint: There at least 12 things that don't belong.

Famous Atlantans of the Past

Atlantans have a long history of community involvement, from their heroic efforts to rebuild their city after the Civil War to the peaceful union of blacks and whites during the civil rights era, to their enthusiasm for hosting the Olympic Games.

- Ralph Emerson McGill won the Pulitzer Prize for his writing urging Atlantans to show goodwill and progress in civil rights for all.
- Martin Luther King Jr. made history in the 1960s as a minister and civil rights leader. He was assassinated in 1968. His tomb is located at the Martin Luther King Jr. Center for Non-Violent Social Change.
- In the arts, Margaret Mitchell is the city's most famous daughter. Her novel *Gone with the Wind* has been translated into many languages throughout the world. A plaque notes the spot on Peachtree Street where, in 1949, she was hit and killed by a taxi.

The tomb of Martin Luther King Jr.

- Civil War heroes are honored throughout the city. You can see the huge carvings of Confederate heroes on Stone Mountain as well as numerous plaques that list the famous battles.

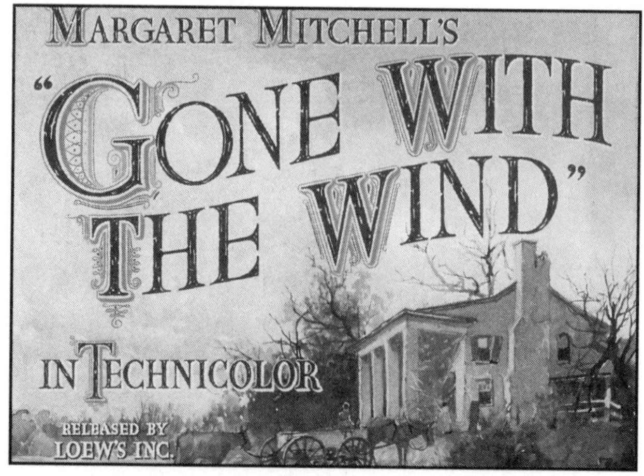

An advertisement for the movie version of *Gone With The Wind*

Greater Atlanta
19
400
Lake
Lanier
River
985
92
75
5
Kennesaw
Mountain National
Battlefield
Park
Chattahoochee
85
400
Powder Springs
Rd
Dobbins
Air Force
Base
285
400
78
78
278
Stone Mountain
Park
River
Piedmont
Park
N
20
Ponce de Leon
Ave
Chattahoochee
285
278
Grant
Park
Hartsfield
Atlanta
International
Airport
285
20
85
75

Famous Atlantans of Today

• Former President Jimmy Carter lived in Atlanta when he was governor of Georgia. The Carter Presidential Center honors his presidency. Carter is now active in working for peace throughout the world. In Atlanta, he and his wife, Rosalynn Carter, can often be seen constructing new homes for Habitat for Humanity, an organization that provides homes for the poor.

• Andrew Young was a congressman, ambassador to the United Nations for Jimmy Carter, and mayor of Atlanta.

• In business, Ted Turner began with a small billboard company and built it into an international communications empire. Other business owners are also helping Atlanta become one of the highest growth areas in new businesses.

• Hank Aaron broke Babe Ruth's home-run record when he played for the Atlanta Braves. He eventually hit 755 home runs and was elected to the Baseball Hall of Fame.

A portrait of former President Jimmy Carter

• Greg Maddux is a contemporary baseball hero. He has won the Cy Young Award for best major league pitcher four times in a row.

Climate

Atlanta's climate is generally mild year-round. The warm days and cool nights in the spring and fall are glorious. Summer can be hot and sticky, but most buildings are air-conditioned and people adapt to the heat. Winter is usually mild, although sometimes it snows or sleets. When that happens, kids listen closely to the weather reports. Atlanta's hills, together with very little snow removal equipment, mean even the slightest hint of bad weather will close the schools. But cold weather rarely lasts long.

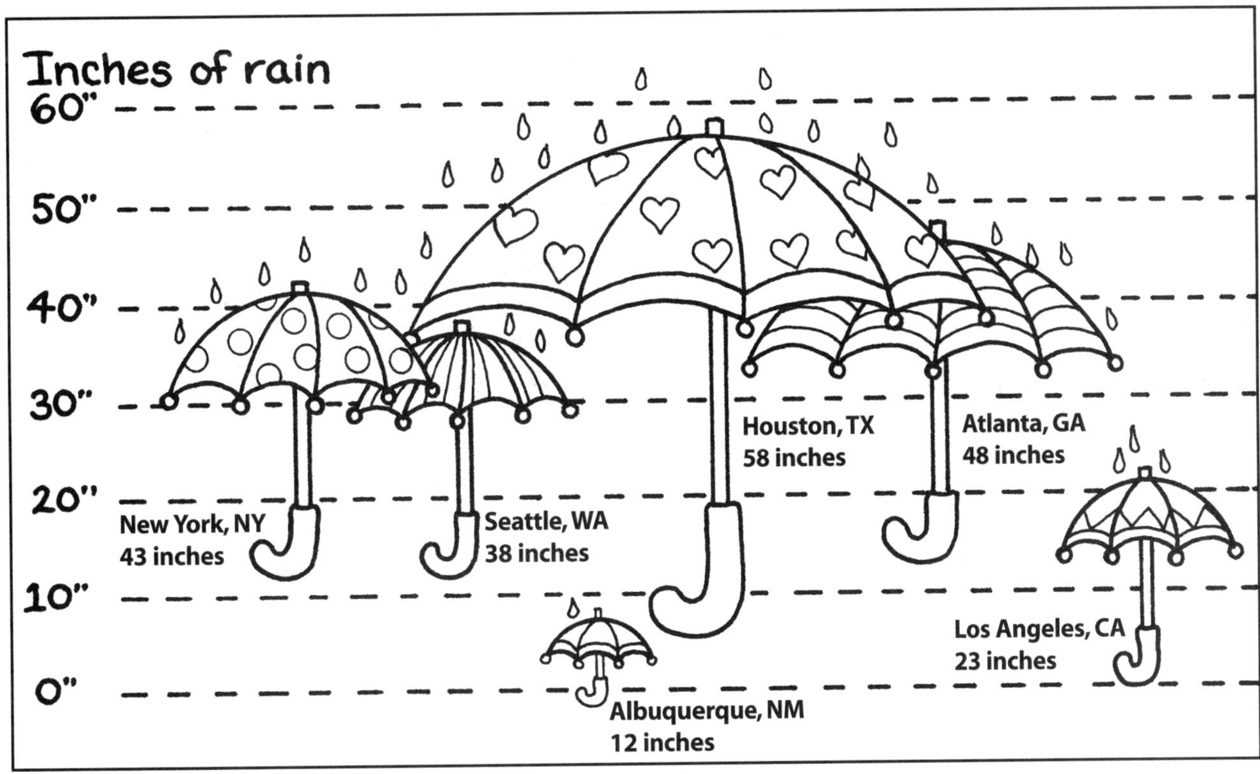

Some people think that Atlanta is always dry. But Atlanta gets more rain than most towns in the United States.

Getting around Atlanta

Atlanta is spread out over a large area, but with lots of expressways and rapid transit systems it's easy to get around. The rapid transit system, called MARTA, is easy to use. MARTA includes buses and trains that reach most locations within the central area of the city as well as some of the suburbs.

The expressway system is simple to navigate. Your parents will discover that I-285 circles the city, I-75 travels northwest to southeast, and I-85 travels from northeast to southwest. I-75 and I-85 join together for a short distance at the Connector in the middle of the city. Outside main tourist areas, a car can be handy—except in rush hour when Atlanta's traffic jams up.

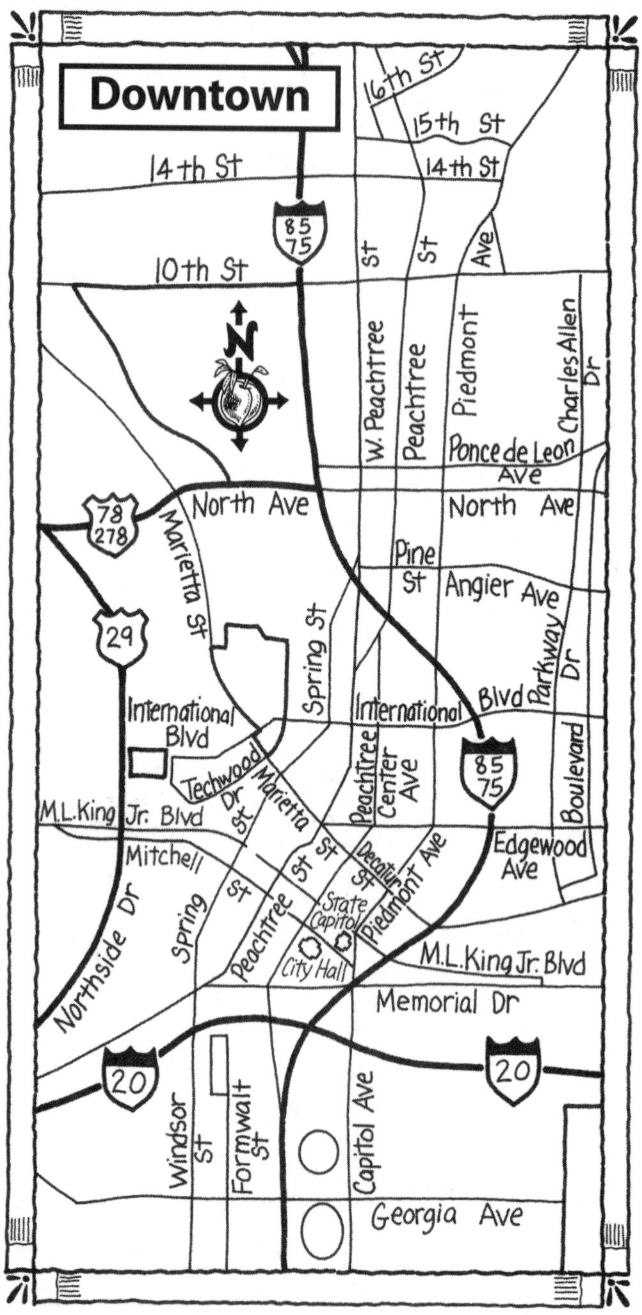

HIDE AND SEEK!

Draw a circle around each hidden object in this drawing of downtown Atlanta. When you're done, color the scene. Look for: a party hat, fork, paintbrush, van, shoe, fish, cowboy hat, comb, hat, camel, apple, butterfly, mushroom, television, pencil, heart, and a baseball bat.

PARKS AND THE GREAT OUTDOORS

THE WHOLE CITY OF ATLANTA LOOKS LIKE A PARK thanks to its huge loblolly pines and flowering plants. Because the weather is mild and often sunny throughout the year, it's the kind of place that makes you eager to spend time outside. That's easy to do in Atlanta. There are hundreds of parks and playgrounds throughout the city and its suburbs. The wandering Chattahoochee River creates dozens of parks just in itself. But even a backyard is fun at night thanks to Atlanta's fireflies. On really good nights, the firefly "show" makes lawns and trees look like they're decorated with hundreds of twinkling holiday lights.

Stone Mountain Park

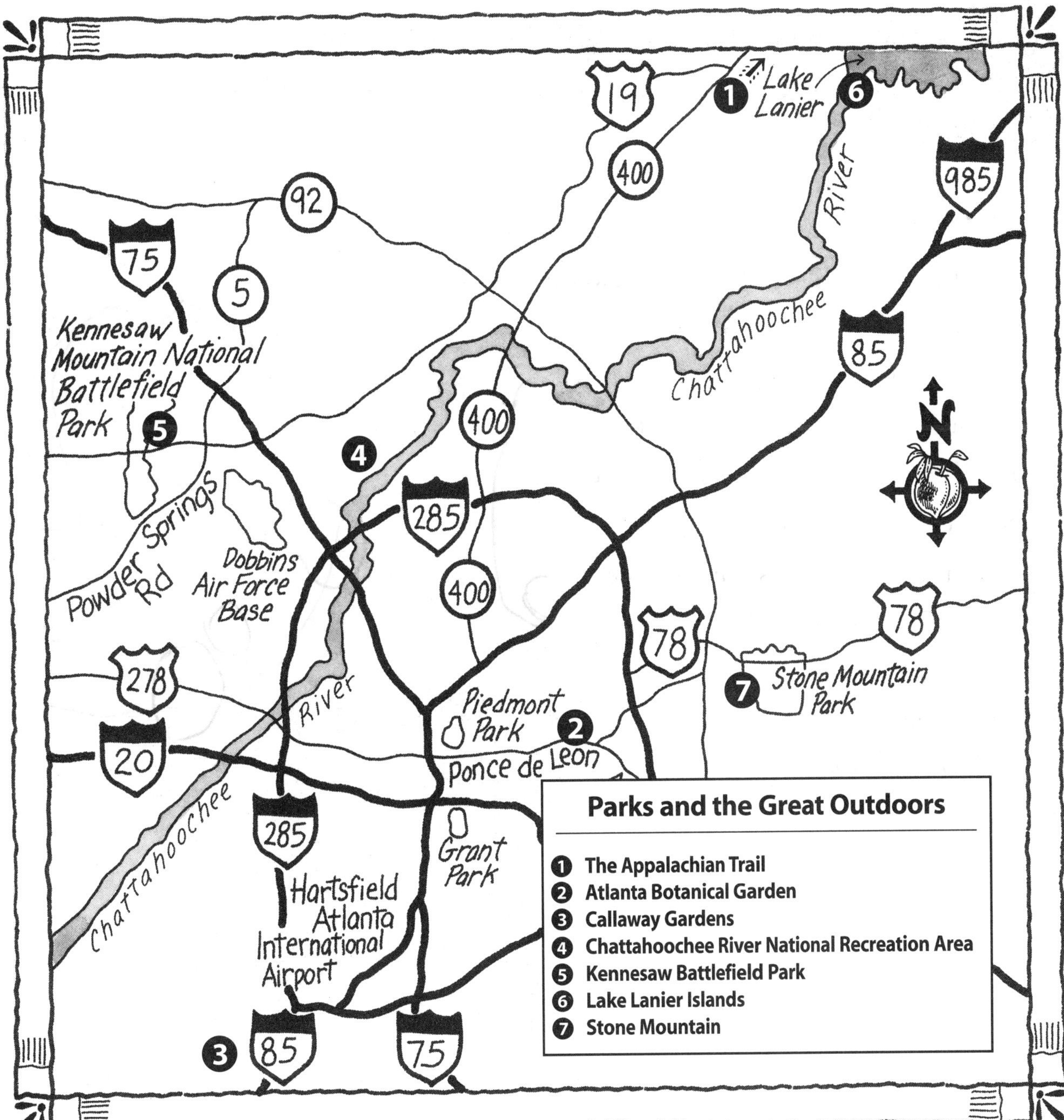
Lake Lanier
19
400
92
985
75
5
Kennesaw Mountain National Battlefield Park
Chattahoochee
River
85
N
400
285
Powder Springs Rd
Dobbins Air Force Base
400
78
78
Stone Mountain Park
278
River
Piedmont Park
Ponce de Leon
20
Chattahoochee
285
Grant Park
Hartsfield Atlanta International Airport
85
75
Parks and the Great Outdoors
1 The Appalachian Trail
2 Atlanta Botanical Garden
3 Callaway Gardens
4 Chattahoochee River National Recreation Area
5 Kennesaw Battlefield Park
6 Lake Lanier Islands
7 Stone Mountain

LAKE LANIER ISLANDS

There are more things to do at Lake Lanier Islands than you can pack into one day—especially in the summer. The **Beach and Water Park** area includes rides galore for all types of swirling, dipping, and sliding fun.

Wildwaves is Georgia's largest wave pool, with over nine different types of waves. For smaller kids, the **Kiddie Lagoon** has tamer "wiggle waves," slides, and water bubblers.

The beach includes $1^{1}/2$ miles of sand for making sand castles and, of course, water to cool off in. You can even skipper a paddleboat, canoe, or sailboat.

Other activities in the park include miniature golf and, at **Lake Lanier Island Stables**, horseback trail rides, pony rides, and lessons. Bike rentals are also available. You can picnic in the park, stop at a snack bar, and pick up a souvenir at the gift shop.

Slipping and sliding at Lake Lanier Islands

Keeping cool in the wave pool

MIXED-UP PICTURE STORY

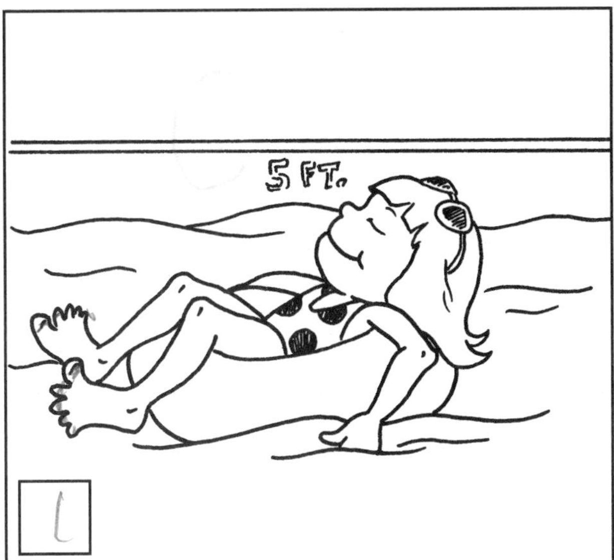

To find out what is happening at the wave pool, put the scene in the correct order by filling in the number box in the bottom corner of each picture.

STONE MOUNTAIN

It took 55 years to finish the granite carving on Stone Mountain, the largest in the world. You've never seen a carving this big! Three Confederate heroes—Confederate President Jefferson Davis and Civil War Generals Robert E. Lee and Thomas "Stonewall" Jackson—ride their horses across Stone Mountain.

Stroll through the **Antebellum Plantation** and imagine what life was like for the people who lived and worked there in the nineteenth century. Tour the elegant **Manor House**, where the plantation owners lived, and visit **Thornton House**, believed to be the oldest restored house in the state.

Stone Mountain Park also offers riverboat rides, a scenic railroad, and a skylift that takes you to the top of the mountain.

The mountainside engraving of Civil War heroes

See the laser shows at Stone Mountain. When it's dark, colorful laser lights and thrilling sound effects make the carved figures "ride" across the mountain.

The skylift at Stone Mountain Park

MOUNTAIN MAZE

These hikers want to go to the top of Stone Mountain. Can you help them get to the skylift before it leaves the station?

CALLAWAY GARDENS

There are all kinds of things to see and do at Callaway Gardens. Thirteen miles of walking trails and scenic drives pass through more than 14,000 acres of gardens and woodlands. You'll see meadows that are bright with flowers and entire trails that seem like a fairyland when the azaleas and rhododendrons are blooming.

Don't miss the **John A. Sibley Horticultural Center**. It's filled with beautiful flowers in a glass building that opens up to the outdoors. Look for the topiaries—sculptures made out of shrubs. You might see dinosaurs, giant bugs, or many other types of animals.

You can walk among the butterflies in the glass-enclosed **Cecil B. Day Butterfly Center** (read more about this in Chapter 3). Or visit **Mr. Cason's Vegetable Garden** and the **Pioneer Log Cabin**. The lake and beach area offers swimming, paddleboating, and miniature golf. Other sports at Callaway include tennis, fishing, and sailboating.

Lush greenery—inside and out

It's a circus all summer when the Florida State University "Flying High" circus performs at the gardens.

Topiary sculpture of a ram

MATCH THE SHRUB SCULPTURE

Every shrub in this garden has an identical twin. After you've drawn a line connecting the matching shrubs, color in the scene.

KENNESAW BATTLEFIELD PARK

This Civil War landmark gives you the feeling that there are soldiers all around. Perhaps that's because the original cannons still rest on top of the mountain. How did they get there? In 1864, General Joseph E. Johnston's Confederate Army dragged them up the steep mountain trails to strengthen their position against Sherman's troops. Johnston's army held the position for two weeks thanks to the cannons and the deep trenches they dug. Both are preserved at the park.

If the weather's clear, the mountaintop gives you a fabulous view of downtown Atlanta and Stone Mountain. You can walk the trails to the top or catch the free shuttle bus.

The park has 16 miles of hiking trails, troop movement maps, monuments, and historical markers. There is a small museum with Civil War exhibits and a film about the battle that was fought here.

On summer weekends, life during the Civil War is re-created through soldier camps, marching, drilling, and other events.

A preserved Civil War cannon

WHAT'S WRONG HERE?

Strange things are happening at Kennesaw Battlefield Park today. Circle at least 15 things you think are wrong with this picture. When you're done, color the scene.

ATLANTA BOTANICAL GARDEN

Have you ever walked through a rainforest? You can, right in the middle of downtown Atlanta. The **Dorothy Chapman Fuqua Conservatory** has a tropical exhibit complete with a waterfall and birds. As you walk up the ramp you're surrounded by exotic tropical plants—palms, ferns, and orchids in amazing colors. You'll even see plants that get their food from the air.

Colorful, exotic flowers thrive at the garden.

For a change of scene, just walk through a door into the **Desert House**. Instantly you go from the moist rainforest to dry desert warmth. Here you'll find weird plants like the lithops (living stones) or the welwitschia, a plant that has no living relatives.

Outside you can explore the rose garden that has more rose varieties than you've ever seen in one place, or rest in the peaceful Japanese garden.

See plants eat insects! Strange but true, some plants you'll see, like the Venus flytrap, trap insects and then digest them.

This striped frog lives in the rainforest.

IN THE GARDEN

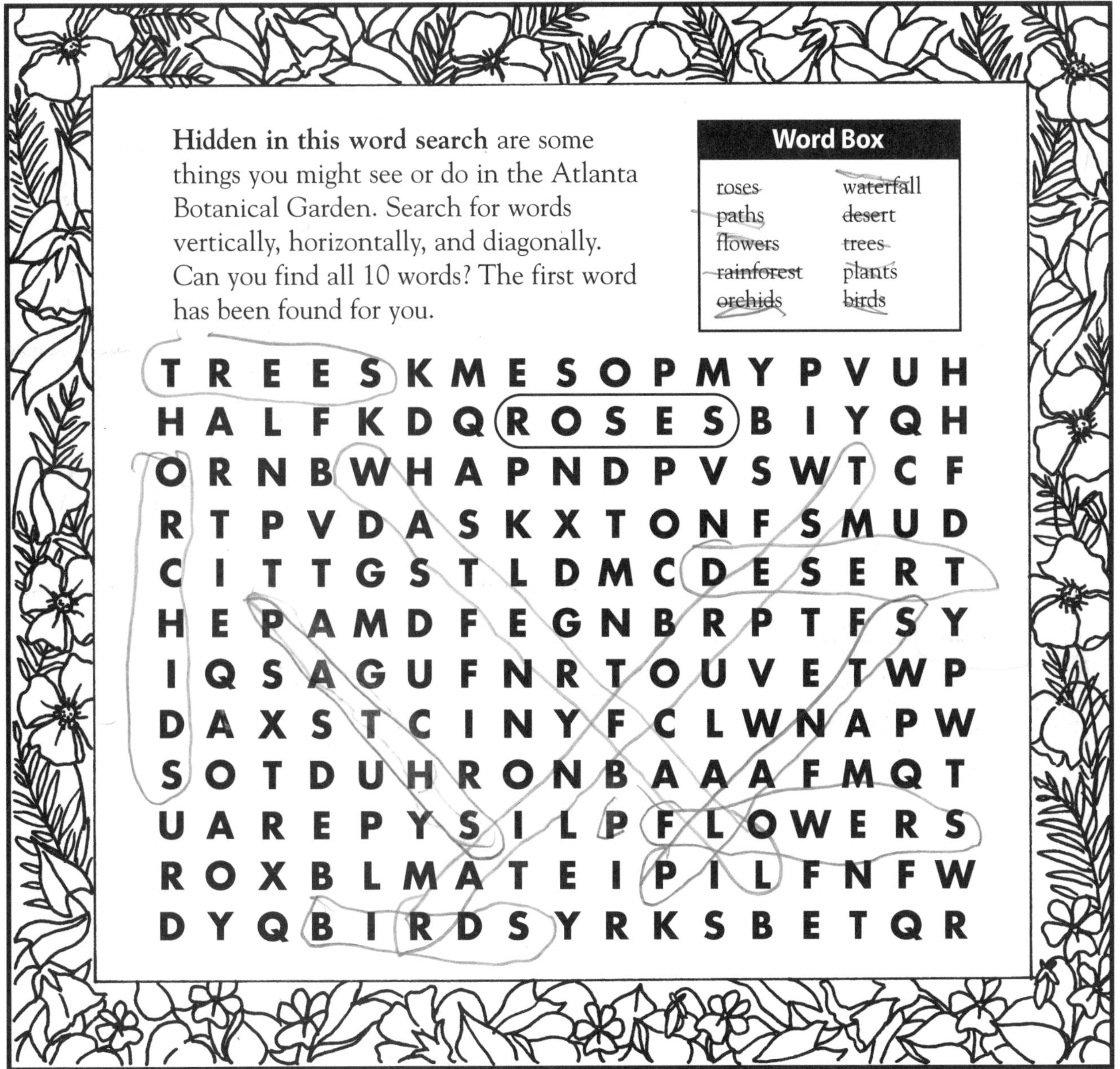

Hidden in this word search are some things you might see or do in the Atlanta Botanical Garden. Search for words vertically, horizontally, and diagonally. Can you find all 10 words? The first word has been found for you.

Word Box

roses	waterfall
paths	desert
flowers	trees
rainforest	plants
orchids	birds

THE APPALACHIAN TRAIL

Fishing at Amicalola Falls State Park

One of Atlanta's greatest outdoor spots isn't in the city at all, but it's only 45 minutes north in the foothills of the Appalachian Mountains. The Appalachian Trail starts in Georgia at Springer Mountain. If you followed it north, you'd eventually end up in Maine—more than six months later! But you don't have to walk that far. You and your family can join the Appalachian Trail at many spots for day hikes. **Amicalola Falls State Park** near Springer Mountain is a pretty place for a picnic, and you can walk up to get a bird's-eye view of the falls.

One especially good hike takes you to **Raven Cliffs**. In the spring, the path is lined with blooming rhododendrons. The hike winds past several small waterfalls and ends at a spectacular waterfall that cascades through a cliff.

Inside the grotto, or cave, below the waterfall you can hop from rock to rock in the stream.

Try your hand at panning for gold or visit the museum on the Dahlonega town square to learn more about Georgia's gold rush.

Panning for gold

WHAT'S IN COMMON?

Each of these waterfalls has something in common with the two others in the same row. For example, the waterfalls in the top row have two levels. Draw a line through each row and describe what the waterfalls in that row have in common. Don't forget to include diagonals!

THE CHATTAHOOCHEE RIVER NATIONAL RECREATION AREA

Atlantans give the Chattahoochee River the nickname "the Hootch," but the river is as long as its real name. It winds its way through Atlanta. There are more than 48 miles of parklands all along the river giving you lots of opportunities for recreation.

You can drift down the river on rafts or tubes. Or rent a canoe and paddle the river while pretending you're a Cherokee Indian. You can also follow the river on walking and jogging paths. At Powers Island, where it seems that all of Atlanta is out for a walk on Sunday mornings, paths are especially popular.

Fishing on the Chattahoochee

Racing down "the Hootch"

Chattahoochee means "painted rock." The name comes from the Cherokee Indians who lived along this river.

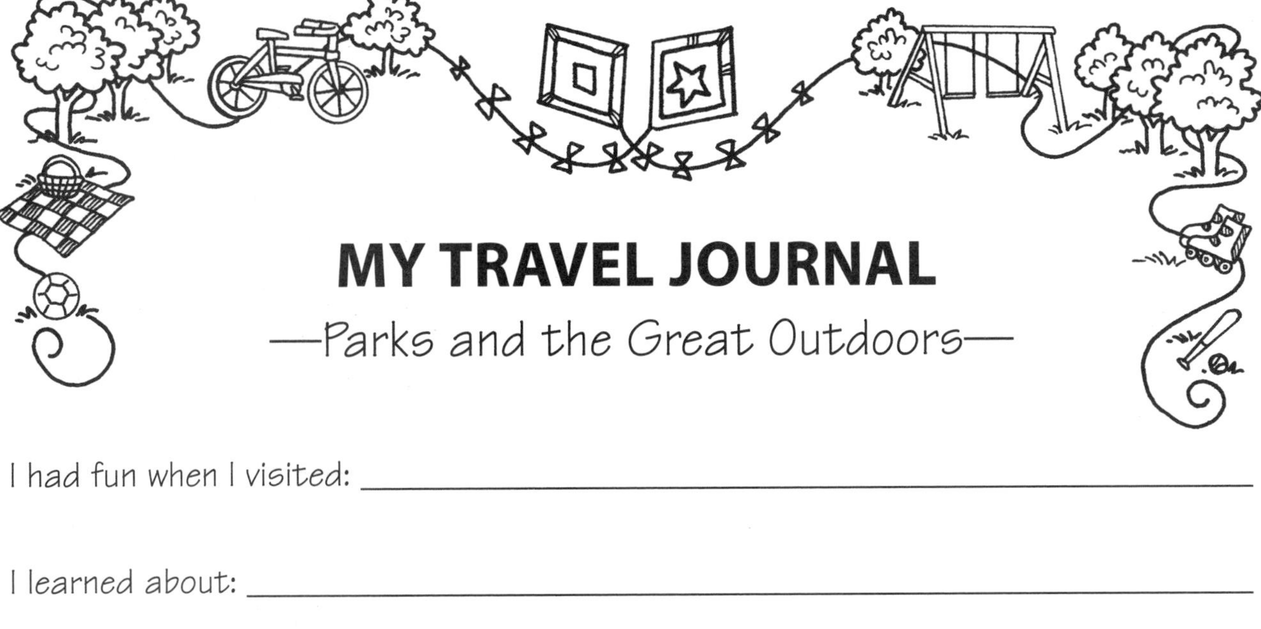

MY TRAVEL JOURNAL

—Parks and the Great Outdoors—

I had fun when I visited: ______________________________

I learned about: ______________________________

My favorite park was: ______________________________

This is a picture of what I saw at a park in Atlanta

3 ANIMALS AROUND ATLANTA

IN ATLANTA YOU CAN ATTEND A BIRTHDAY PARTY for a gorilla, watch a butterfly perch on your shoulder, or visit the famous groundhog who predicts the end of winter. Atlanta's zoos and game parks are special places for animal watching, but you can see many of Atlanta's animals just by being outdoors. The Chattahoochee River and nearby woods make an ideal home for beavers and ducks. Atlanta's tall trees are home to birds that greet the morning with caws and songs. Atlanta even has eagles roosting in the skyscrapers downtown!

The biggest recent news was the black bear cub that wandered down into an Atlanta suburb from the mountains north of the city. Don't worry, though. The cub is safely back at its home.

A crowned crane at Zoo Atlanta

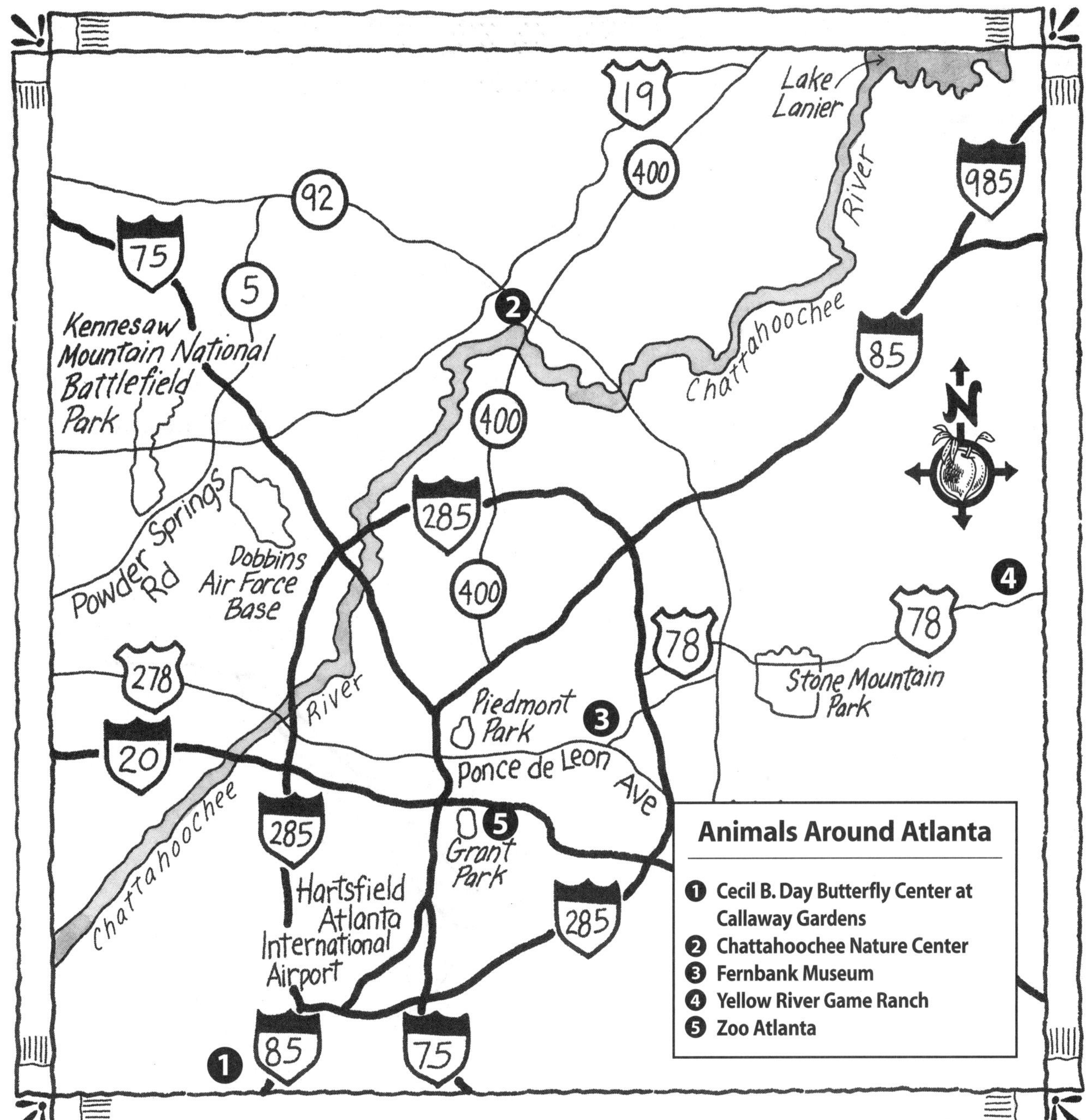

19
Lake Lanier
400
92
985
75
5
2
River
Kennesaw Mountain National Battlefield Park
Chattahoochee
85
400
Powder Springs Rd
Dobbins Air Force Base
285
400
4
78
78
278
Piedmont Park
3
Stone Mountain Park
River
20
Ponce de Leon Ave
285
5
Grant Park
Chattahoochee
Hartsfield Atlanta International Airport
285
1
85
75
Animals Around Atlanta
1 Cecil B. Day Butterfly Center at Callaway Gardens
2 Chattahoochee Nature Center
3 Fernbank Museum
4 Yellow River Game Ranch
5 Zoo Atlanta

ZOO ATLANTA

More than 1,000 animals live here, most of them in habitats designed to look like their natural homes. The most famous resident is Willie B the gorilla. He even has an official birthday party every year. Willie B lives in the **Ford African Rain Forest** with four gorilla families. You can see him up close during feeding time, when he poses for visitors.

The **Masai Mara** is a re-creation of the East African plains where giraffes, zebras, ostriches, and antelope roam freely. Rhinos, lions, and even elephants splash in their watering hole nearby.

Pet the goats, baby llamas, pigs, and sheep at the **Children's Zoo**. Or watch one of the naturalists' shows to learn more about the animal activities you've seen. Enjoy popcorn and peanuts from the refreshment stand, but feed yourself, not the animals!

A great way to see the zoo without walking is to take the train. It drops you off at various points along the way.

Willie B, the zoo's most famous resident

An African lion

Without telling anyone what you're doing, ask for a word to fill in each blank. For example, "Give me an action word." When all the blanks are filled in, read the story out loud. One of the blanks has been filled in for you.

Willie B liked __________ (action word) ing the visitors who came to see him. He especially __________ (emotion) ed watching the zoo train go by. "I wish I could ride the train," he said to himself one day. "It looks so __________ (describing word). That night Willie sneaked out into the zoo. When he found the __________ (thing), Willie climbed in and put on the conductor's hat. He __________ (action word) the train all around the pond (place). "Hop in," he called to the other animals each time he __________ (action word). The next morning the conductor was very __________ (emotion) when he stopped the train in front of Willie's enclosure. " __________ (exclamation)!" he exclaimed. "How did Willie get my __________ (thing)?"

WILLIE B ON THE LOOSE!

CHATTAHOOCHEE NATURE CENTER

What's that splash? Is it a beaver scurrying away down the river? Or maybe it's a duck diving, rear end up, for a bit of cracker you've thrown from your canoe. If you're a city kid, the Chattahoochee Nature Center in Roswell, just north of Atlanta, is the place to explore woodlands, ponds, and the Hootch—the Chattahoochee River.

You can paddle the river in a guided canoe tour to see beaver lodges, animal tracks, plants, and birds. Or wander down the nature trails to learn about native plants and animals. Then visit the raptor and reptile exhibits.

A bald eagle

Exploring pond life at the Nature Center

CANOEING IN THE HOOTCH

These canoeists on the Chattahoochee River want to find their way back to the Nature Center. Can you help them? When you're done , color in the scene.

FERNBANK MUSEUM

Dinosaurs are extinct, but you'll love the way they come to life here. The walls at Dinosaur Hall are covered by bright murals, or paintings, of the different dinosaur eras. In the main room, giant dinosaur replicas tower over museum visitors.

Don't miss "**A Walk Through Time in Georgia.**" As you stroll from room to room, you'll see different habitats as well as native Georgia animals such as alligators, raccoons, and egrets.

Children's Discover Rooms include the **Fantasy Forest**, for children ages three to five, and **Georgia Adventure**, for ages six to ten. These areas have hands-on exhibits that teach about nature. **The World of Shells** has a unique seashell display and a 1,000-gallon living-reef aquarium.

The IMAX Theatre shows exciting films that make you feel like you're in the middle of the action—riding the Space Shuttle, drifting across the ocean floor, or migrating with wildebeests across the Serengeti Plain.

Eons ago dinosaurs lived in the area.

Find the fossils at your feet. The floor tiles here are made of limestone from a German quarry. They contain fossils that are 150 million years old!

Murals and models bring these extinct creatures to life.

CROSSWORD FUN

There is a lot to do at the Fernbank Museum. Solve this crossword by figuring out the clues or completing the sentences. If you need help, use the clue box.

Across

2. Animals or plants that are preserved in rock are called ________.
3. When the last animal of its kind dies, that animal is ________.
6. You can keep fish in an ________.
7. The World of Shells has a display of these.
8. The place where an animal live is called its ________.

Clue Box

shuttle	fossils
extinct	IMAX
shells	aquarium
habitat	touch
fantasy	

Down

1. This theater shows exciting films on a huge screen.
2. The ________ Forest is really a room that teaches kids about nature.
4. To feel something, you use your sense of ________.
5. The astronauts ride this into space.

CECIL B. DAY BUTTERFLY CENTER

Have you ever had a butterfly perch on your shoulder? It just might happen at the Cecil B. Day Butterfly Center. As you walk along the paths in this glass enclosure, you can watch butterflies flit through the air or sit on the semitropical and native plants around you. This butterfly conservatory is the largest in North America. It has over 1,000 free-flying tropical butterflies with 70 different butterfly species, including some from Asia, South America, and Africa.

One of the most popular activities is watching butterflies emerge from their cocoons, called the chrysalid stage. The chrysalids are in display cases, but when they mature and change into butterflies, the keeper releases them right where you stand.

When you arrive, watch the short film about the butterfly life cycle. If you have any questions, just ask one of the volunteers in the Center.

The Butterfly Center

A butterfly sipping nectar

To attract butterflies, wear a bright color like red. The butterflies might think you're a big flower and land on you!

WHAT'S THE DIFFERENCE?

These two pictures of the Butterfly Center might look the same, but they are not. How many differences between the two scenes can you find? Hint: There are at least 15 differences.

YELLOW RIVER GAME RANCH

A donkey nuzzles a visitor at the ranch.

When you walk into this ranch, you'll be given special animal food. Then you can feed and pet some of the 600 animals and birds along the trail at this 24-acre nature park.

Georgia's official weather forecaster lives here. He's the groundhog General Lee, who lives in his own "mansion" complete with swimming pool and satellite dish. If General Lee sees his shadow on Groundhog Day, February 2nd, Atlantans are in for another six weeks of winter.

For *Babe* fans, there's a farm area where you can get nose-to-nose with goats, sheep, donkeys, chickens, pigs, and geese.

The wooded areas are home to deer, buffalo, bear, cougars, fox, raccoons, and other wild animals. At **Billy Goat Gruff Memorial Bridge** the goats climb above you to be fed.

One Saturday in May, the sheep get sheared, or shaved. You can help, and later you can watch the wool being spun into yarn on a spinning wheel.

MY TRAVEL JOURNAL

—Animals Around Atlanta—

I had fun when I visited: ______________________________

I learned about: ______________________________

____

My favorite animal was: ______________________________

This is a picture of an animal I saw

LANDMARKS, SKYSCRAPERS, AND THE ARTS

"EVERYTHING IS SO NEW!" one young visitor said when she first saw Atlanta's skyline. Yes, everything does seem new here. That's because after its destruction in the Civil War, Atlanta was rebuilt from the ground up. Today, giant cranes work to build even more skyscrapers as the city grows.

Downtown Atlanta skyscrapers

You can see art everywhere in Atlanta. Besides the many formal museums, art can be discovered in the most amazing places along the streets and in the parks. Atlanta's art runs from sculptures selected for the Olympics to children's drawings decorating the fence around a hospital.

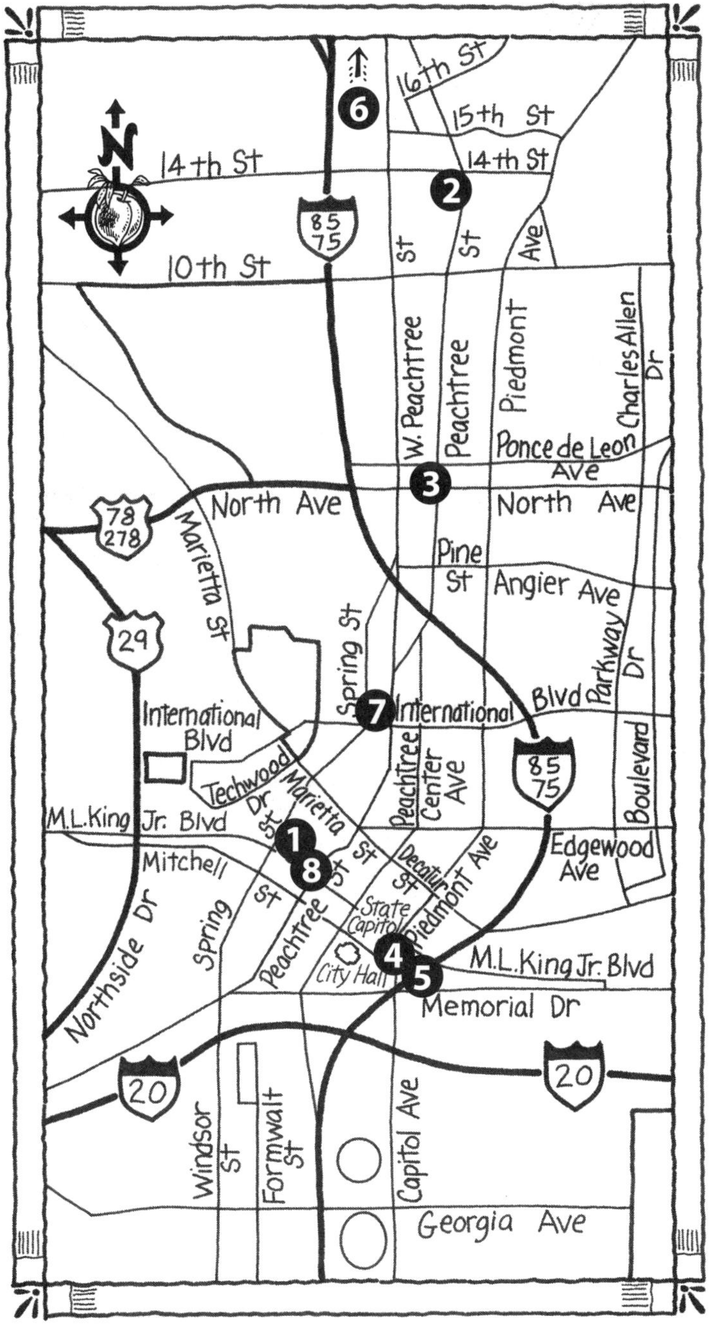

Landmarks, Skyscrapers, and the Arts

1. Atlanta Heritage Row Museum
2. The Atlanta Memorial Arts Center
3. The Fox Theatre
4. Georgia State Capitol
5. Georgia State Museum of Science and Industry
6. Governor's Mansion
7. Peachtree Center
8. Underground Atlanta

ATLANTA MEMORIAL ARTS CENTER

The Arts Center is actually several buildings that contain art, theater, and music facilities. You'll recognize the **High Museum**, part of the Arts Center, because it's very unique. The building is bright white with lots of glass and curves. From the street you'll see spots of red, yellow, and white bobbing around a black triangle—a giant mobile by Alexander Calder, a famous sculptor.

Inside, the atrium's high glass ceiling lets in lots of natural light. It's fun to walk up the ramp that circles up, up, up to the galleries on different floors. The museum has contemporary and traditional art, plus examples of decorative arts like furniture and ceramics.

The High Museum

The atrium is light and airy.

In Symphony Hall you can listen to concerts by the world-famous Atlanta Symphony. The Alliance Children's Theater plans shows especially for kids.

DRAW YOUR OWN MOBILE

A mobile is a sculpture that moves when the wind blows. If you had the chance to make your own mobile, what would it look like? Draw your mobile on this page, then color in the scene.

PEACHTREE CENTER

Peachtree Center includes shops, office towers, hotels, and restaurants—and they're all connected by a series of tunnels and glassed-in overpasses. It's like a giant maze. You can even stand right over the street and watch the traffic flow under you.

Peachtree Center has its own MARTA train station. It's carved out of the rough granite directly below the center.

Get a bird's-eye view of Atlanta from the top of the **Westin Peachtree Plaza.** This is the tallest hotel in North America. It's 723 feet tall and has 72 stories. Ride up in one of the glass elevators just for the view. At the top you can eat in the restaurant, or use the telescopes on the viewing platform for a look at the entire city.

The Peachtree Center MARTA station across from the Atlanta Public Library has the longest escalator in the Southeast. At a steep 190 feet, it's easier if you don't look down!

The l-o-o-o-ng escalator at the MARTA station

At the top of the Westin Peachtree Plaza

WHAT'S WRONG HERE?

Today is an odd day at the mall. Circle at least 15 things that you think are wrong with this picture. After you're done, color the scene.

THE FOX THEATRE

You'll see the most amazing sky *inside* the Fox Theatre. Look up when you enter the auditorium. The ceiling is covered with twinkling stars, moving clouds—even a sunrise and sunset. The auditorium itself looks like something out of a stage set. With its flashy, gold-tone decorations and red velvet curtains, it's no wonder this theater is known as "the fabulous Fox." It's one of the most important landmarks in Atlanta and it's on the National Register of Historic Places.

The lobby of the Fox Theatre

You can join a tour to see behind the scenes and hear all about the Fox. Or go to one of the shows. The Fox hosts a range of entertainment including musicals, concerts, and classic films.

Mickey Mouse began here. The Fox Theatre opened as a movie house on Christmas Day in 1929. It was one of the first theaters to show Walt Disney's original Mickey Mouse cartoon, *Steamboat Willie*.

Inside the fabulous Fox

A TRIP TO THE THEATER

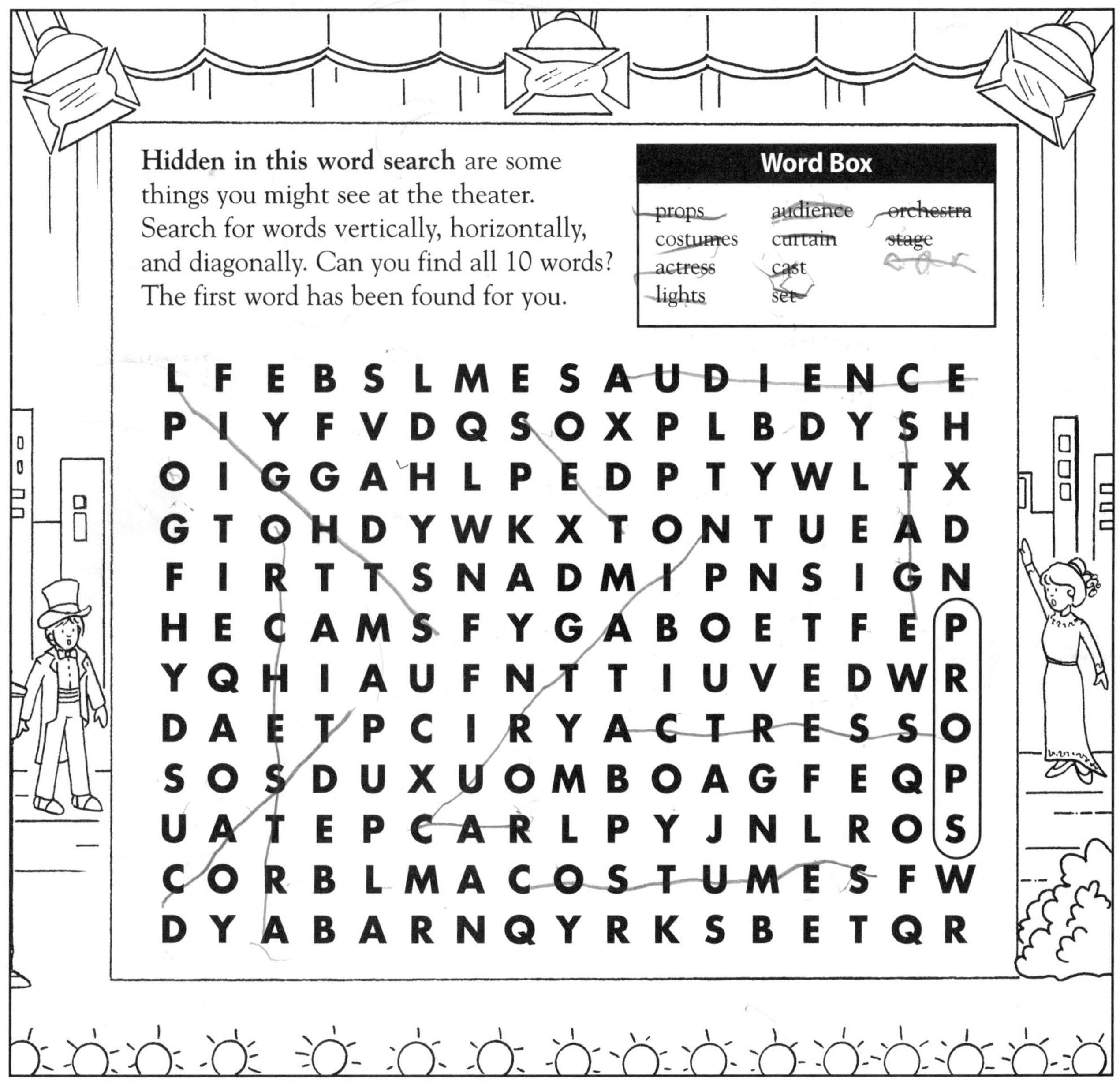

UNDERGROUND ATLANTA

Street performers in Underground Atlanta

This is the area where Atlanta began. In the 1920s, the main street and railroad tracks were covered over by elevated roads, called viaducts, so that cars could drive overhead. The original streets and buildings were buried! But not anymore. The entire six-block area is now designed for people to walk around in—no cars allowed. The area is filled with over 120 shops, restaurants, and entertainment areas. It's a great place to shop for souvenirs. When you're tired, the food court will refresh you with a cold drink or a light meal.

At the **Atlanta Heritage Row Museum** you can learn about the history of Atlanta through interactive exhibits, displays, and maps. Some exhibits let you imagine you're the pilot of a jet approaching Atlanta's Hartsfield International Airport. Or you can hear a famous speech by Dr. Martin Luther King Jr. while you stand at his lectern, see the drama of the Civil War up close, and so much more.

A SHOP OF YOUR OWN

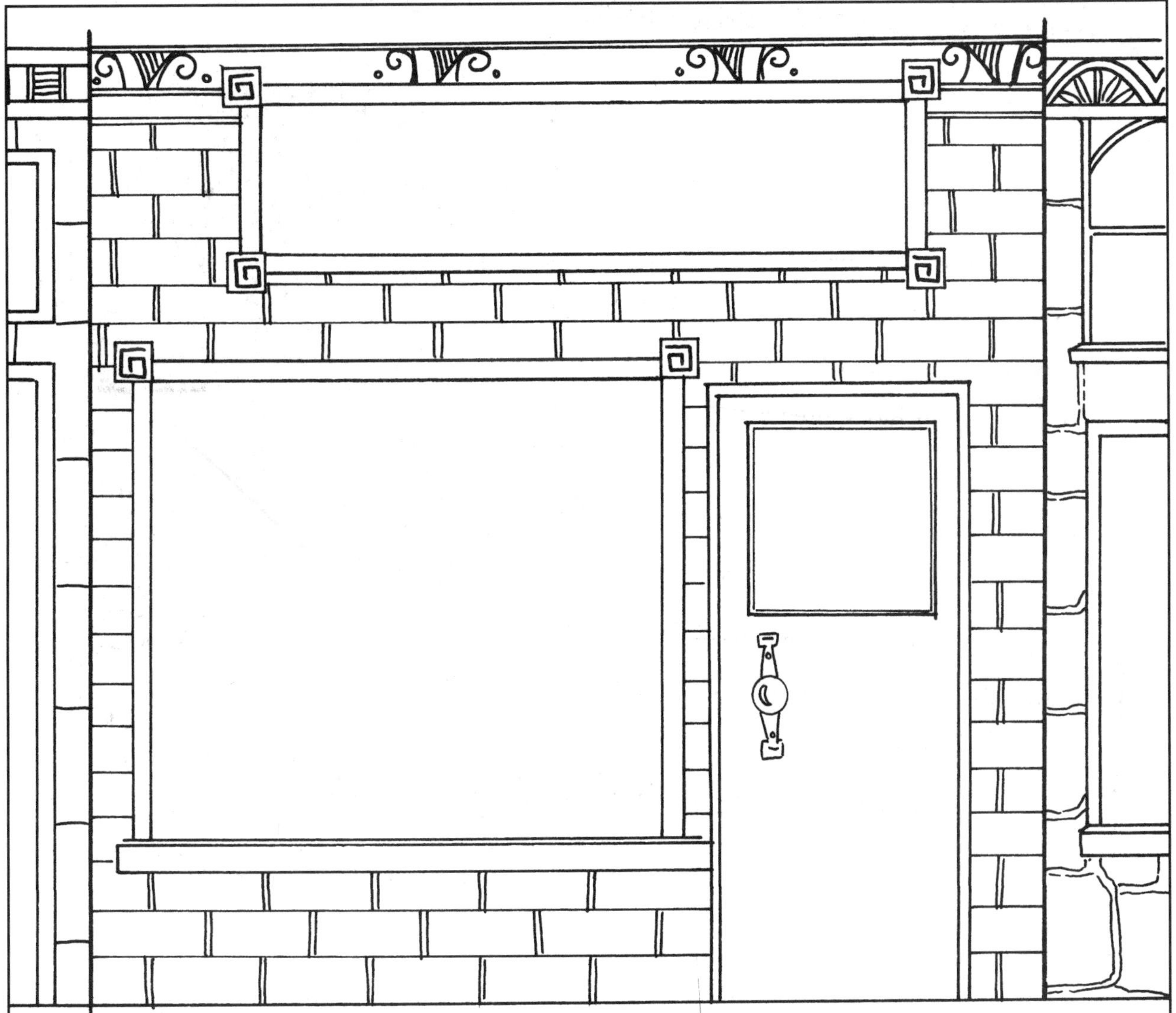

If you could open your own shop in Underground Atlanta, what would it be called and what would you sell? Write the name of your shop on the sign above. What would you display in the windows to attract shoppers? Draw your display in the shop window.

GEORGIA STATE CAPITOL

When you're downtown, look for the shiny gold dome. That's the Georgia State Capitol. Atlanta became the capital of Georgia in 1868, but the building wasn't actually completed until 1884. The builders brought the gold leaf for the dome from Dahlonega, a city in the mountains just north of Atlanta.

Bet you didn't know that the very first gold rush in the U.S. was in 1828, in Dahlonega, Georgia.

Inside, the Capitol houses offices for state officials, and it also contains the **Georgia State Museum of Science and Industry**. This isn't a big museum, but it has some very interesting exhibits. You'll love the Indian heritage exhibit. It shows how the Native Americans in this area lived over 2,500 years ago. You can also see exhibits on Georgia's natural history and native wildlife, including the two-headed snake, and displays of local rocks and minerals.

The Georgia State Capitol

A GOLD ROOF FOR THE CAPITOL

Without telling anyone what you're doing, ask for a word to fill in each blank. For example, "Give me an action word." When all the blanks are filled in, read the story out loud. One of the blanks has been filled in for you.

Prospector Pete and his partner, ___________ (name 1), had been ___________ (action word)ing for some gold in the hills (place). "It's time we took this gold to town," said Pete. When they got to Atlanta, the ___________ (describing word) Brandi Belle ___________ (action word)ed to greet them. "You'd better hide that gold," said Brandi. "There's a thief in town." "___________ (exclamation)!" said Pete "This gold is too ___________ (describing word) to carry around, but I can't let it out of my sight."

Suddenly he had an idea. "Come on, ___________ (name 1)," said Pete.

The next day Brandi saw where Pete had put his gold.

"What a capitol idea," she laughed.

GOVERNOR'S MANSION

Many trees bloom on the grounds of the Governor's Mansion each spring.

The governor of Georgia lives in this beautiful, colonial-style mansion. You can take a tour of the house and the gardens around it on certain days of the week. The beautiful furnishings inside include paintings, furniture, and porcelain sculptures—many of them from the nineteenth century.

A lot of people forget to see the grounds, but they are worth a look. There's a sculpture garden on one side of the mansion. In spring, you can see a beautiful display of color and blossoms on the many azaleas and dogwood trees.

The mansion's elegant porch

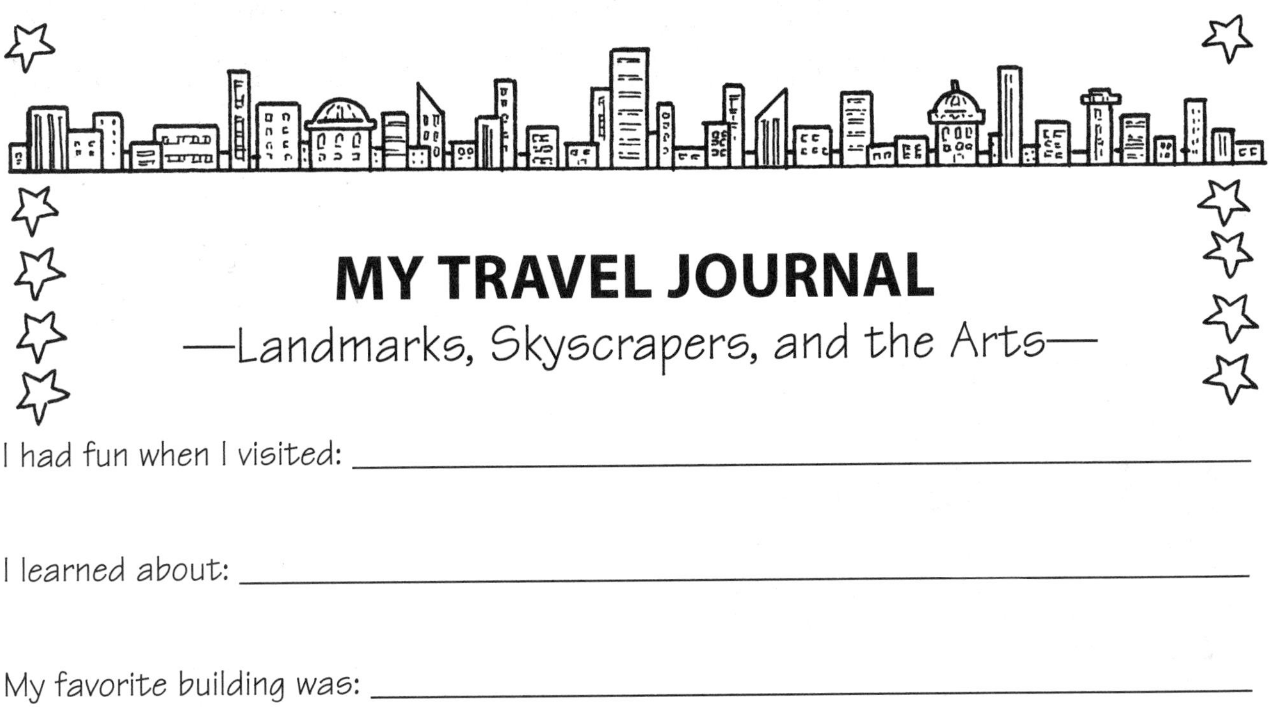

MY TRAVEL JOURNAL

—Landmarks, Skyscrapers, and the Arts—

I had fun when I visited: ______________________________

I learned about: ______________________________

My favorite building was: ______________________________

This is a picture of a building I saw

GOOD SPORTS

ATLANTA HAS HOSTED THE GREATEST GATHERING of athletes ever—the Centennial Olympic Games, so it's a terrific place to enjoy sports.

People throughout the Southeast cheer for Atlanta's professional sports teams in baseball, football, hockey, and tennis. They often do more than cheer on others, though, because Atlanta makes it easy to enjoy a wide range of sports. You can do anything from rafting down the Chattahoochee River to playing tennis on countless numbers of courts.

Within the city, you can jog, skate, swim, or fly kites in parks. Nearby, hike Stone Mountain, Kennesaw Mountain, or the Appalachian Trail. If you still want more, go whitewater rafting, hot-air ballooning, or horseback riding. You name it—the sports activities are all here, just for the fun of it.

A player takes a "bubble break" at an Atlanta Lawn Tennis Association match.

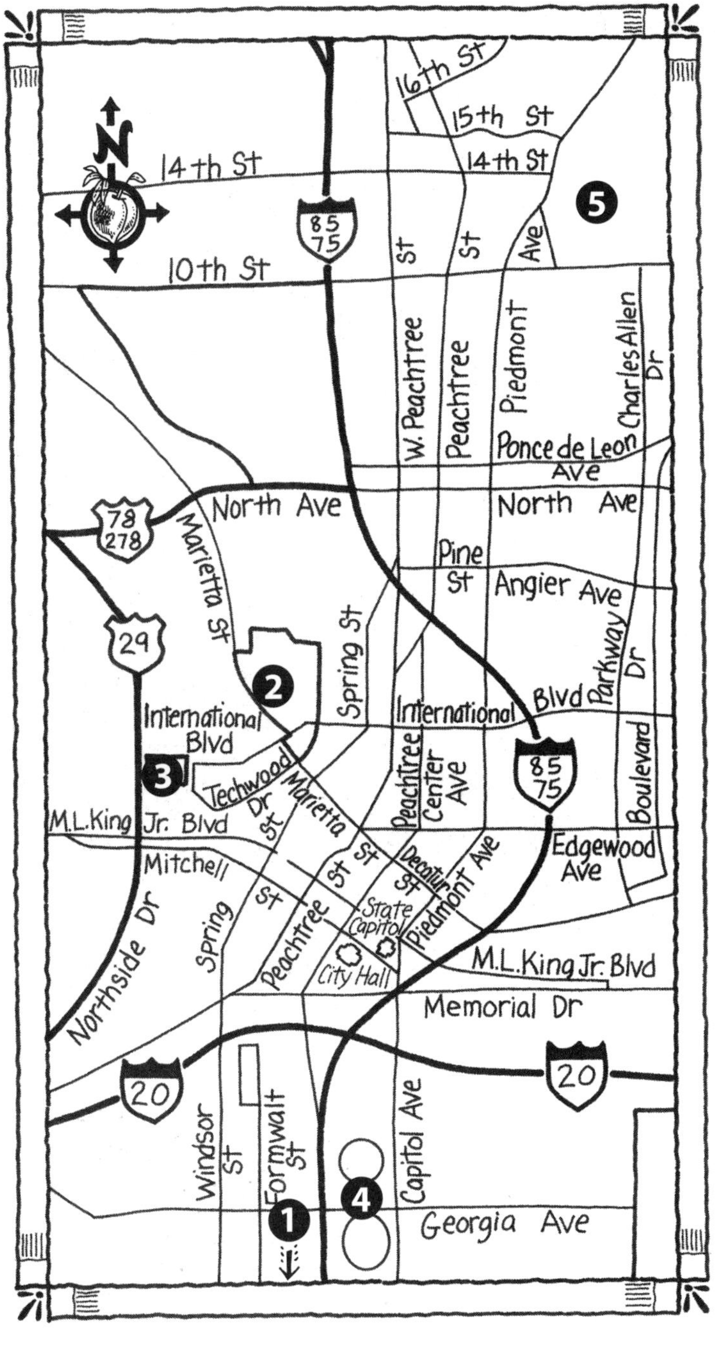

Good Sports

1. Atlanta Motor Speedway
2. Centennial Olympic Park
3. Georgia Dome
4. Olympic Stadium
5. Piedmont Park

CENTENNIAL OLYMPIC PARK

This park was built for the Centennial Olympic Games in 1996. The city of Atlanta hosted athletes from around the world in the largest sports competition ever held. Atlanta's Olympics had participation from more countries and more athletes than ever before. Thanks to Centennial Olympic Park, everyone got to participate in the Olympic fun, even if they didn't have tickets. It was—and still is—a gathering place right in the middle of Atlanta.

Atlanta's newest gathering place

The Olympic Rings Fountain spouts water shaped like the five interlocking Olympic rings. It's designed to be a playground for kids. The water retreats into the ground so you can walk inside, then watch the water spring up to create a cage around you. You're not supposed to get wet when you're inside the ring, but the splashing is part of the fun.

Olympic Rings Fountain

CROSSWORD FUN

There are lots of things to see and do at Olympic Park. Solve this crossword by figuring out the clues or completing the sentences. If you need help, use the clue box.

Clue Box

clap	centennial
sports	playground
pen	Olympic
tickets	train
Atlanta	

Across

1. To go to the Olympic games, people had to buy these.
4. The Olympic Rings Fountain is meant to be a ________ for kids, but it doesn't have swings or slides.
7. What athletes do to get ready for an event, or something you might ride on a trip.
8. You can use one of these to fill in this puzzle.
9. What you do to cheer on an athlete or team.

Down

2. The 100th birthday of something, or part of the name of Atlanta's new park.
3. Swimming, baseball, and gymnastics are different kinds of ________.
5. Where you're visiting if you bought this book.
6. At the ________ Games, athletes from all over the world try to win medals.

ATLANTA BRAVES

The Braves made history with their miraculous "worst to first" season in 1991. That was when they won the National League Championship and a trip to the World Series. It was one of several remarkable seasons. The Braves have kept their title as National League champions for several years in a row and have been to the World Series three times since 1991.

Known in Atlanta as "America's Team," the Braves originally played in the Atlanta Fulton County Stadium. Their new home is **Olympic Stadium**, the site where the 1996 Olympic Games' opening and closing ceremonies, plus track and field events, were held. It was converted into a baseball stadium especially for the Braves, and it provides a view of Atlanta's skyline for the seated fans.

The Braves used to play baseball at Fulton County Stadium.

Olympic Stadium

The Braves' original home, Atlanta Fulton County Stadium, was called the "Launching Pad" because so many home runs were hit there.

WHAT'S THE DIFFERENCE?

These two pictures of an Atlanta Braves game might look the same, but they are not. How many differences between the two scenes can you find? Hint: There are at least 15 differences.

ATLANTA MOTOR SPEEDWAY

Getting ready for a race

Vrooooom! Thirty miles south of Atlanta, the cars go even faster than they do on the expressways. On race days, the noise here is intense, and so is the excitement. If you like cars, you'll love **Road Atlanta** and the Atlanta Motor Speedway.

These are two of the best racing facilities in the country. Road Atlanta hosts exciting drag racing and stock-car events. Atlanta Motor Speedway hosts and offers the largest stock-car racing prize on the NASCAR circuit. It holds events such as the NASCAR Winston Cup, the Motorcraft 500, and the NASCAR Busch Grand National.

You can take a tour to see behind the scenes, including a visit to Pit Road and the NASCAR garage where million-dollar machinery is fine-tuned.

The gift shop here is a racing fan's dream come true. It's packed with Atlanta Motor Speedway and Winston Cup caps, clothing, and collectibles.

Atlanta Motor Speedway

RACING MAZE

Help the race car driver find his way from the starting line to the checkered flag. When you're done, color in the scene.

ATLANTA FALCONS

Atlanta's NFL football team is the Atlanta Falcons. Their home is the **Georgia Dome**. From the outside, the dome looks like a giant marshmallow, but the puffy white roof is actually the world's largest cable-supported domed stadium in the world. The roof is covered by a fiberglass fabric coated in Teflon that's strong enough to support a fully loaded four-wheel-drive pickup truck. It's as tall as a 27-story building.

The Georgia Dome is the most state-of-the-art football stadium in the country. It includes closed-circuit television, a large-screen video system that shows replays, and teleconferencing capabilities.

The 1994 Super Bowl, the annual Peach Bowl, and the 1996 Olympic basketball games and gymnastics competition were held here. Other sporting events, concerts, and trade shows also take place here.

You can tour the Dome to see the stadium, Astroturf storage room, press box, the executive concourse and suites, and other areas.

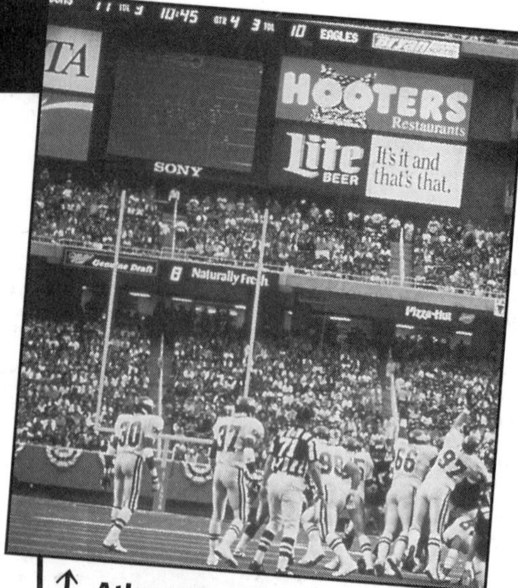

Atlanta Falcons

Dome power! It takes 16,400 kilowatts of electricity to operate the Dome—enough to light up a small city.

Georgia Dome by night

FOOTBALL FEVER!

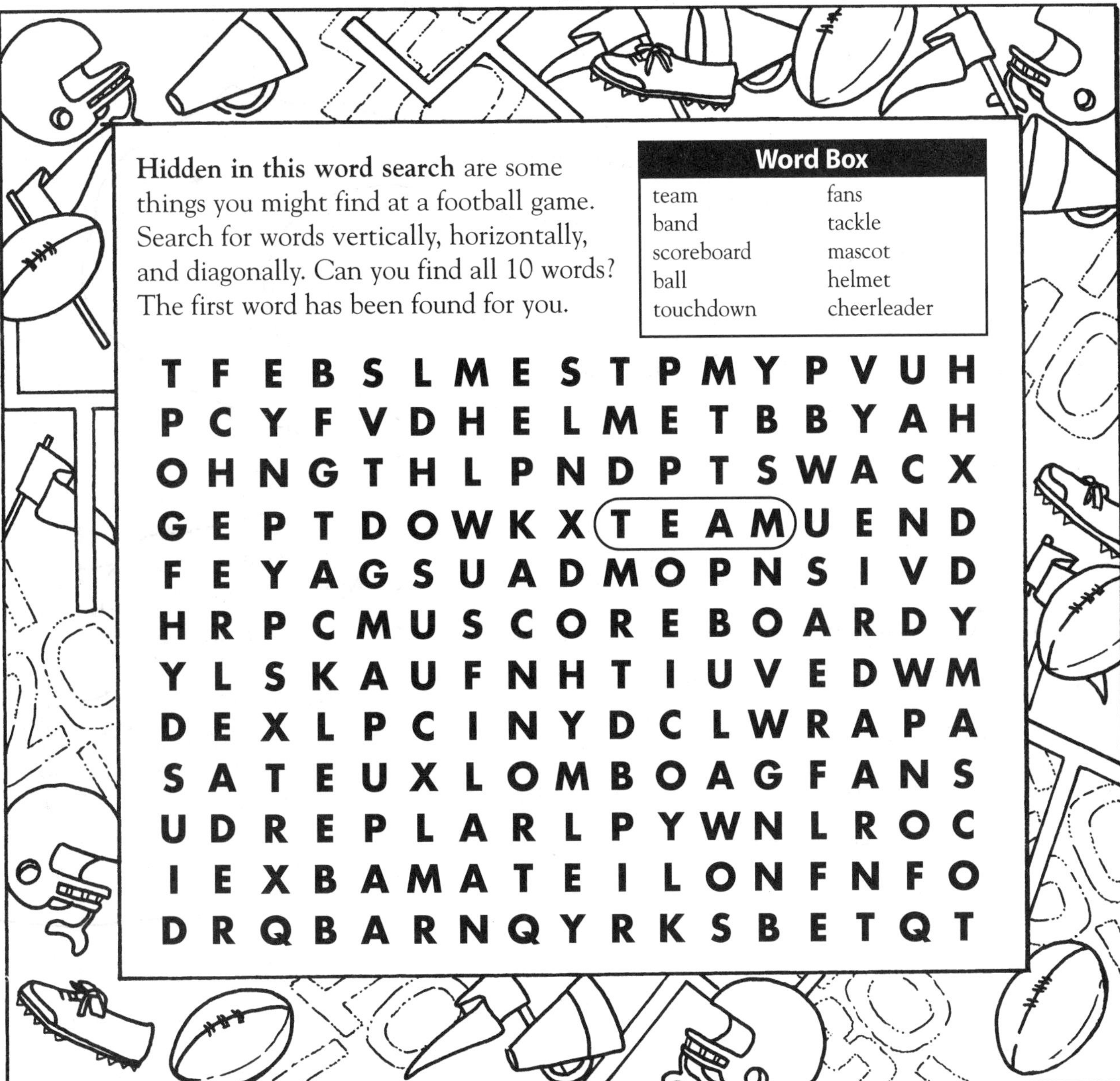

Hidden in this word search are some things you might find at a football game. Search for words vertically, horizontally, and diagonally. Can you find all 10 words? The first word has been found for you.

Word Box	
team	fans
band	tackle
scoreboard	mascot
ball	helmet
touchdown	cheerleader

```
T F E B S L M E S T P M Y P V U H
P C Y F V D H E L M E T B B Y A H
O H N G T H L P N D P T S W A C X
G E P T D O W K X(T E A M)U E N D
F E Y A G S U A D M O P N S I V D
H R P C M U S C O R E B O A R D Y
Y L S K A U F N H T I U V E D W M
D E X L P C I N Y D C L W R A P A
S A T E U X L O M B O A G F A N S
U D R E P L A R L P Y W N L R O C
I E X B A M A T E I L O N F N F O
D R Q B A R N Q Y R K S B E T Q T
```

PIEDMONT PARK

Go fly a kite on the grassy hill overlooking the park. Or in-line skate, jog, bike, or walk on the paths that wind through the park. Whenever it's a nice day, Piedmont Park is the best spot in town to spend time outdoors.

You can rent in-line skates, roller skates, or bikes at **Skate Escape** across Piedmont Road at 12th Street. It's easy to find—just look for the beginning skaters holding on to lampposts! Meanwhile, the "experts" who show up at the park every week zip around, showing off their technique. If you're nice, they'll give you tips on how to stop or circle.

Watch for news of concerts, art fairs, or other special events to be held here. This is the place to be entertained and to people watch.

Each year on July 4, Piedmont Park is the finish line for the Peachtree Road Race. With 50,000 runners, it's the largest 10-kilometer (6-mile) race in the world.

Kids playing in Piedmont Park 

MY TRAVEL JOURNAL

—Good Sports—

I had fun when I visited: ______________________________

I learned about: ______________________________

My favorite sport is: ______________________________

I like it because: ______________________________

This is a picture of something I saw

MUSEUMS AND MORE

FROM THE CIVIL WAR TO A CIVIL RIGHTS HERO, Muppet puppets to a famous soft drink, or dinosaurs to space travel, Atlanta's museums seem to have it all. Many museums have hands-on exhibits where you can try experiments yourself. You can take guided tours or explore on your own. Whether you like major exhibits brought from around the world or small, fascinating displays from local areas, there's a lot to see at Atlanta's museums.

The giant neon bottle at World of Coca-Cola

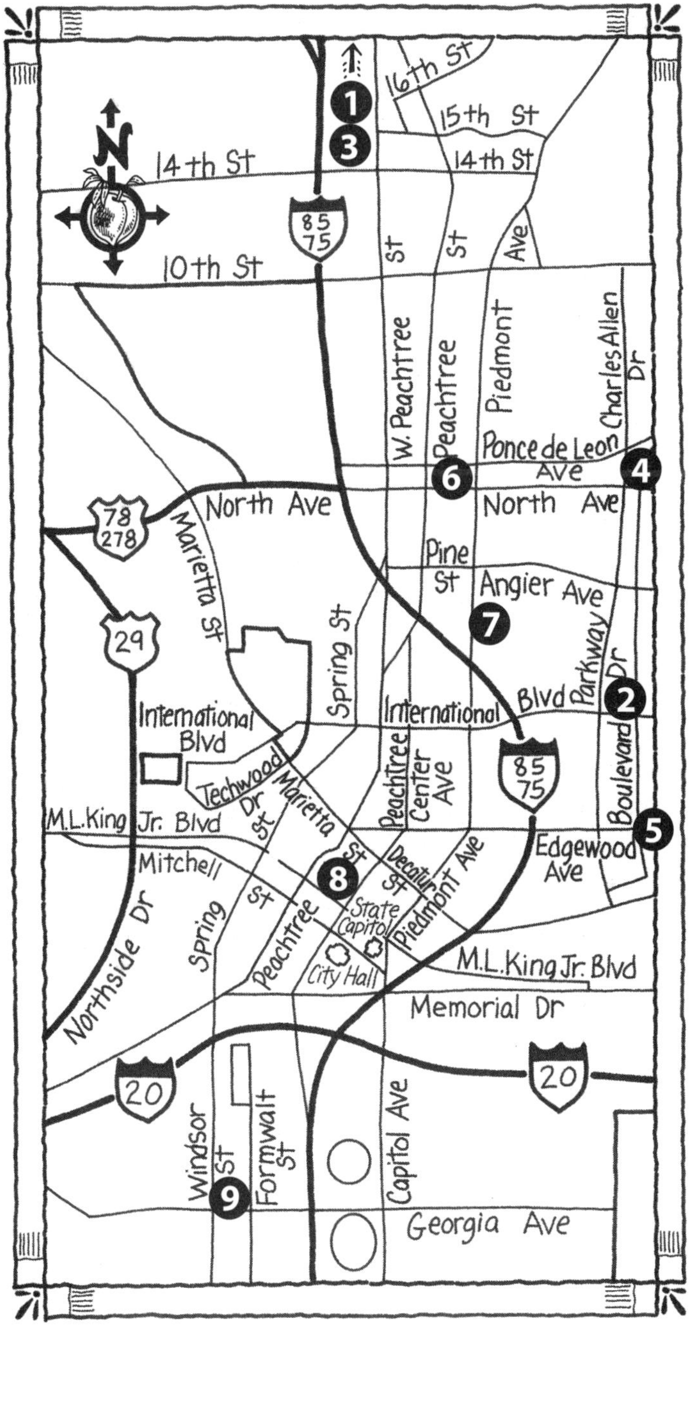

Museums and More

1. Atlanta History Center
2. Carter Presidential Center
3. Center for Puppetry Arts
4. Fernbank Science Center
5. Martin Luther King Jr. Center
6. Road to Tara Museum
7. SciTrek
8. The World of Coca-Cola
9. The Wren's Nest

ATLANTA HISTORY CENTER

Here's where you can discover all about Atlanta—its earliest days, the Civil War and the Reconstruction that followed it, and its modern development as an international city.

The **Atlanta History Museum** lets you discover the Civil War and other events in Atlanta history. Try lifting the heavy knapsack and musket Confederate soldiers had to carry. Look for swan decorations throughout the **Swan House**. Tour it to see how Atlanta's richest people lived in the early twentieth century. Or go further back in time at the **Tullie Smith Farm**. This 1840s house and farm shows what life was like before the Civil War. You can see displays of traditional crafts, a blacksmith shop, the vegetable and herb garden, and even farm animals.

↑ The Tullie Smith house

On the weekend closest to July 22, the anniversary of the Battle of Atlanta, visit the Civil War camp. "Confederate soldiers" cook out, perform rifle exercises, and do other tasks typical of the time.

Swan House →

WHAT DOESN'T BELONG?

This is a scene you might have witnessed during the Civil War. But you'll notice many things that didn't exist back then. When you find something that doesn't belong, circle it. Then color in the scene. Hint: There are at least 12 things that don't belong.

THE WORLD OF COCA-COLA

People from more than 195 countries drink Coca-Cola, and this museum gives you a taste of the product and its history. The museum includes a large collection of Coca-Cola collector's items. Some of them are displayed around a fascinating moving sculpture that's a light-hearted look at the bottling process.

The **Pause that Refreshes** is an imitation of a 1930s soda fountain. The "soda jerk" shows how the drink was prepared before modern equipment. You can listen to original songs about Coca-Cola as well as re-broadcasts of old-time radio programs on a genuine 1930s jukebox.

Club Coca-Cola is the most radical soda fountain you'll ever see. You can sample exotic drinks from around the world in the **International Video Lounge** while you watch international TV commercials.

Video exhibits at World of Coca-Cola

The International Video Lounge

Coke, the world's most popular soft drink, was created in Atlanta in 1886. It was first sold at a drugstore as a remedy for headaches.

THE NEWEST SOFT DRINK

Without telling anyone what you're doing, ask for a word to fill in each blank. For example, "Give me an action word." When all the blanks are filled in, read the story out loud. One of the blanks has been filled in for you.

Professor ____________ (girl's name) had worked on her experiment for __________ (number) days. She wanted to invent a soft drink that didn't go flat. "I must find a way to keep the __________ (things) in my soda pop," she said. The professor ________ (action word)ed her ingredients to the beaker, then she turned on the carbonation _________ (thing). When the soda was ready, she poured it into a green (describing word) bottle and capped it tightly. The next day, the professor opened the bottle and drank the soda. The soda was so fizzy, her hair ________ (action word)ed.

" ___________ (exclamation)!" she burped.

"This is _____________ (describing word) fizzy pop!"

THE CENTER FOR PUPPETRY ARTS

This is one of Atlanta's unique museums, and it's the largest facility devoted to puppets and puppet performances. Even your parents will enjoy wandering among the wide variety of puppets. The displays cover over 200 puppets from around the world including formal African figures, European marionettes (wooden figures moved by string), the famous Punch and Judy characters, shadow puppets from Thailand, and some Jim Henson Muppets like the stars of *Pigs in Space*.

You can try moving puppets yourself at special interactive stations. Or watch the puppet shows put on by the Center's puppeteers or by visiting companies from all over the world.

Sign up at the Center for a puppetry workshop where you can create your very own puppet to take home.

Kids making puppets of their own

A young visitor moves a puppet with special controls.

THE LONELY PUPPET

One puppet in this show doesn't have an exact match. Draw a line connecting the matching puppets to find the one without a twin.

ROAD TO TARA MUSEUM

This museum is dedicated to *Gone with the Wind*, Atlanta's most famous book. It's a favorite throughout the world and it has been translated into 28 languages. The **Rare Books and Manuscript Room** holds autographed first editions as well as foreign editions of the book—even Japanese!

In the **Costume Gallery** you can see reproductions of original gowns and uniforms from the movie, including Scarlett's "drapery dress" and Melanie's wedding dress. **David O. Selznick's Screening Room** shows films on Margaret Mitchell's life and on the Battle of Atlanta.

One whole wall in the museum is covered by more than a hundred different *Gone with the Wind* dolls in beautiful costumes. The walls are also decorated with original posters and photographs from the making of the movie.

Visit the gift shop for collectibles, posters, and Atlanta souvenirs.

When Margaret Mitchell first wrote *Gone with the Wind*, she titled it "Road to Tara." That's where the name of this museum comes from.

An original movie poster

Dolls of Scarlett O'Hara and Rhett Butler 

A classic scene from the movie version of *Gone with the Wind*

FERNBANK SCIENCE CENTER

Dinosaur Hall

This science center is full of things to see and do. Go star gazing at the **Planetarium**. It's one of the largest in the country. You'll be entertained by the shows and on clear evenings, the observatory is open so you can view the night sky.

In the exhibit hall, you can see replicas of prehistoric dinosaurs that lived in the area, as well as animals and birds native to Georgia. Then climb a few stairs for a close-up look inside an Apollo 6 space capsule. Yes, it's the real thing, complete with re-entry burns on the side. There's a space suit on display, too.

A geological video lets you in on the secrets of volcanoes, earthquakes, and mountain formations.

On a nice day, follow the nature trails and watch for turtles sunning themselves on logs in the ponds.

This Planetarium exhibit shows what the earth looks like from space.

CROSSWORD FUN

Solve this science museum crossword by figuring out the clues or completing the sentences. If you need help, use the clue box.

Clue Box

planet
clear
stars
prehistoric
outer space
turtle
earthquake

Across

1. If you take a ride in the Apollo 6, you are probably traveling to ________.
3. At the Planetarium, you'll see fun shows about these.
4. Dinosaurs lived during this time.
7. The earth is one of these.

Down

2. When this happens, everything shakes.
5. You might see one of these slow animals on a nature trail.
6. The best time to see stars is on a ________ night.

MARTIN LUTHER KING JR. CENTER

Martin Luther King Jr. Center

Dr. King, the civil rights leader and winner of the Nobel Peace Prize, is honored here with exhibits on his life. The museum includes exhibits on the civil rights era along with Dr. King's personal possessions, such as his ministerial robe. His marble tomb is outside.

The neighborhood where the Center is located is known as the **Sweet Auburn** district. It was home to successful black-owned businesses and entertainment, and the pride of black Atlanta in the mid-1890s. Today it's the location of many other black historic sites. For example, one block west of the Martin Luther King Jr. Center you'll find the **Dr. Martin Luther King Jr. Birth Home**. Dr. King was born here on January 15, 1929, and spent his first 12 years here.

Ebenezer Baptist Church was where Dr. King served as co-pastor, just like his father and grandfather had. Dr. King preached his first sermon here at age 17.

Dr. King's birthplace

Learn more about Atlanta's black history and neighborhoods at the African American Panoramic Experience (APEX).

CARTER PRESIDENTIAL CENTER

Get an inside look at life in the White House. The **Museum of the Jimmy Carter Library** includes an exact replica of the Oval Office the way it looked when Mr. Carter was president. You can see a formal dinner setting from the White House and several events at the executive mansion that were videotaped.

Can you imagine the fabulous gifts that the president of the United States receives? You can see many of them in a display that ranges from handmade gifts from the American people to lavish objects from foreign leaders, such as a silver falcon from the Kingdom of Saudi Arabia.

Carter Presidential Center

A unique interactive video display includes a modern "town hall" that lets you ask Jimmy Carter questions. Try this one: what did Amy do all day at the White House?

The interactive video Town Meeting exhibit

Outside the Center, there's a pretty Japanese garden surrounding a pond.

SCITREK

No one will tell you "hands off" in this museum! Georgia's Science and Technology Adventure ("SciTrek" for short) provides tons of touchable exhibits and experiments so you can try your hand at learning all sorts of fun facts. Over 150 permanent exhibits show you how things work, including light and color recognition, electricity, magnets, and mechanical gadgets. There's even an area called **Kidspace** for the smallest kids (ages two to seven). You can see amazing performances that highlight the laws of science—and this real-life knowledge is even better than a magic show!

No time to visit Paris? Look for the Eiffel Tower at SciTrek. It's smaller, but it's an exact replica of the original.

Visitors explore color and light in this SciTrek exhibit.

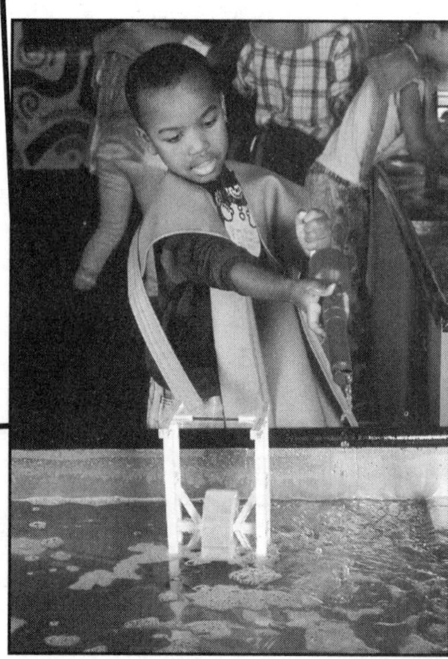

Hands-on learning about water power

WHAT'S WRONG HERE?

It's a strange day at the museum and lots of things are out of place. Circle 10 things that you think are wrong in this picture. When you're done, color in the scene.

THE WREN'S NEST

Some people collect stamps or coins. Joel Chandler Harris collected African American folktales for 25 years. He heard lots of folktales when he worked on a plantation, and he wrote the stories down so people would remember them for years to come. The stories include characters who have become famous, such as Uncle Remus, Br'er Rabbit, Br'er Fox, and all their other animal friends.

The Wren's Nest is a museum and a national historic landmark. The Victorian home is furnished the way it was when Mr. Harris and his family lived here, so you can see his books, photographs, and private collections. You can also see a diorama, or miniature exhibit, from Walt Disney's *Song of the South*, the movie made about the stories.

You can join one of the special storytelling sessions, picnic on the grounds, or shop for souvenirs in the museum shop.

Wren's Nest, the home of Br'er Rabbit's creator

A room in the historic house

Most of the Uncle Remus tales came directly from African folklore. 'Br'er' means brother and 'Sis' means sister in the folklore.

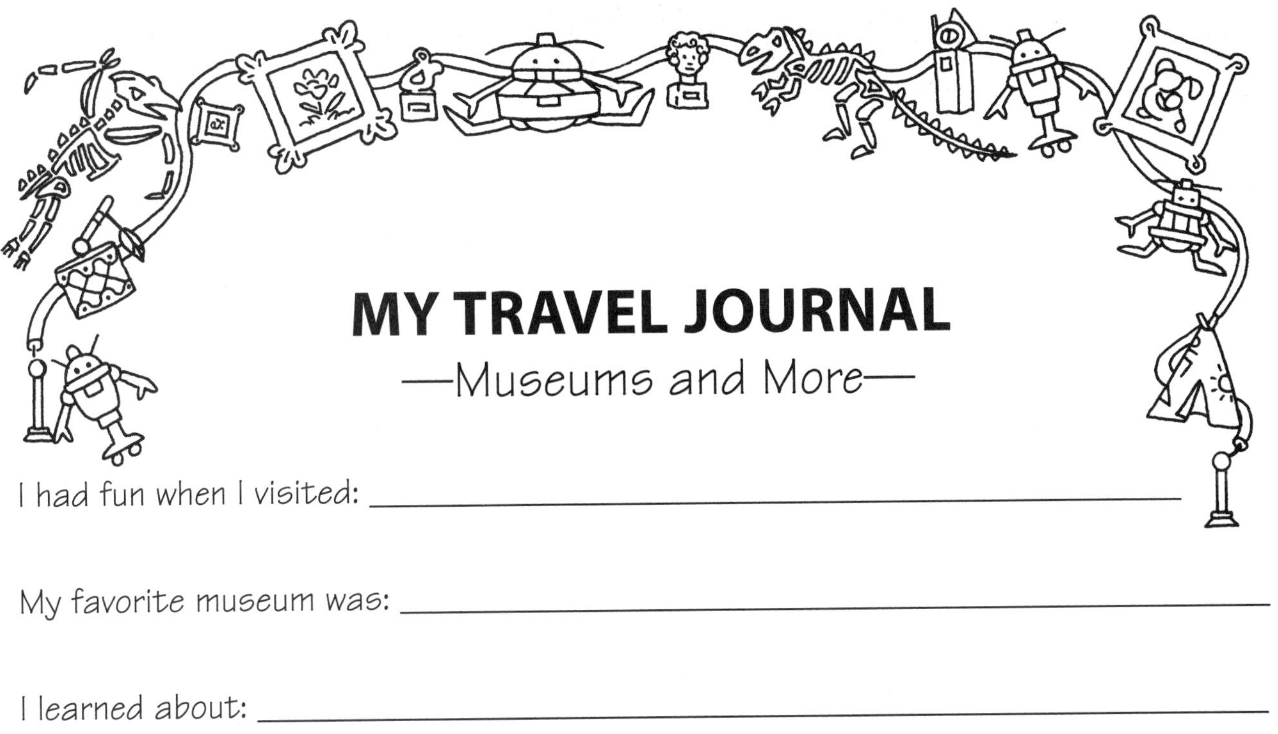

MY TRAVEL JOURNAL

—Museums and More—

I had fun when I visited: ______________________________

My favorite museum was: ______________________________

I learned about: ______________________________

This is a picture of a painting or sculpture I saw

THAT'S ENTERTAINMENT

INDOORS AND OUT, YOU'LL FIND HUNDREDS of entertaining things to do in Atlanta. Ride the waves for cool fun at a water park or watch a play at a children's theater. Zoom up, down, and all around on rides at one of Atlanta's amusement parks during the day. At night, settle down to watch the laser show light up Stone Mountain.

The *Atlanta Journal and Constitution* lists each week's special activities in the Saturday pullout section. See the Resource Guide in the back of this book for events throughout the year, as well as important phone numbers you can call for more information.

A train chugs up the mountain at Stone Mountain Park.

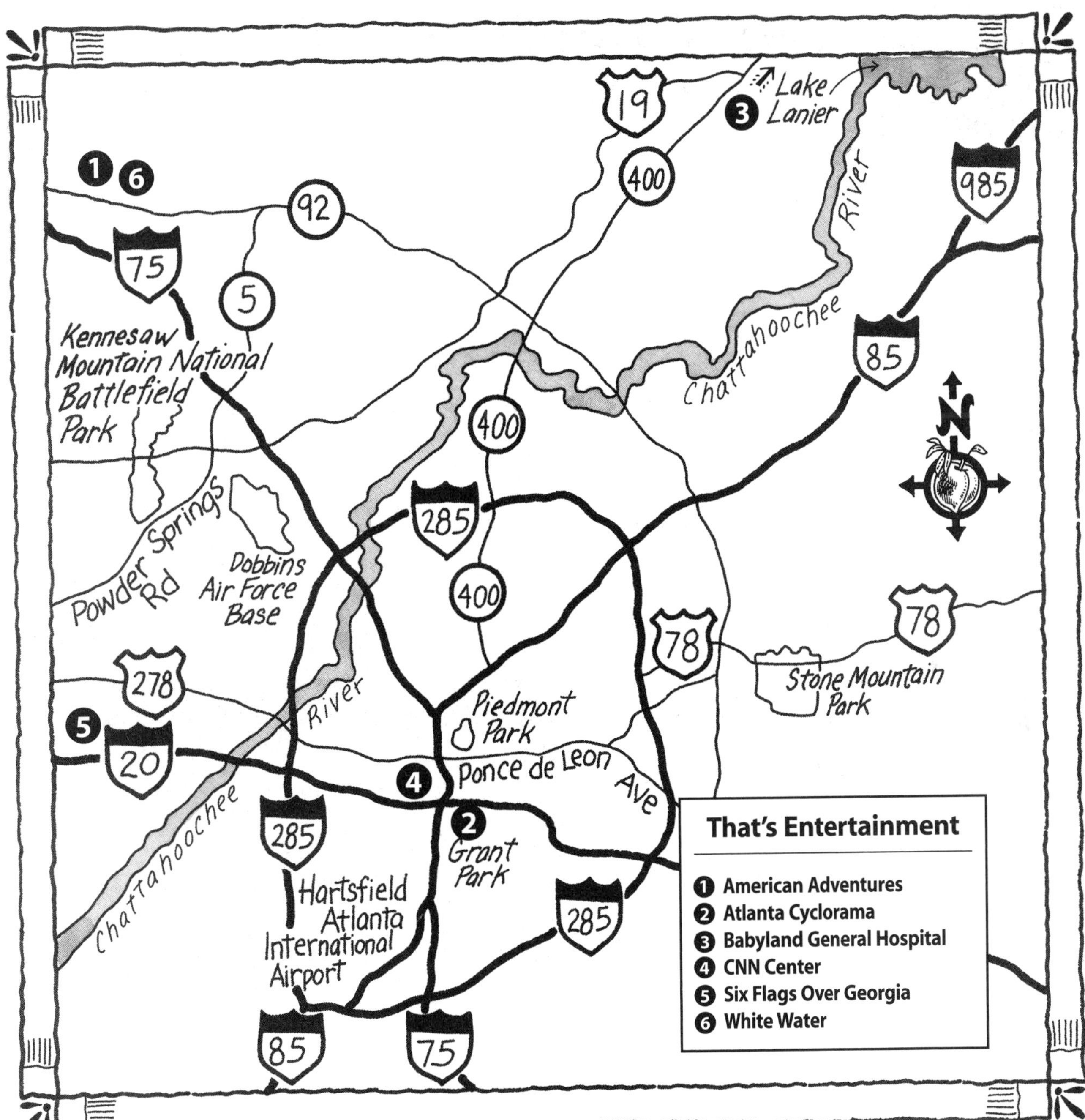

19
Lake Lanier
3
1 6
92
400
985
River
75
5
Kennesaw Mountain National Battlefield Park
Chattahoochee
85
400
Powder Springs Rd
Dobbins Air Force Base
285
400
78
78
Stone Mountain Park
278
Piedmont Park
River
5
20
4
Ponce de Leon Ave
Chattahoochee
285
2
Grant Park
Hartsfield Atlanta International Airport
285
85
75
That's Entertainment
1 American Adventures
2 Atlanta Cyclorama
3 Babyland General Hospital
4 CNN Center
5 Six Flags Over Georgia
6 White Water

WHITE WATER

This is wow on water! When the weather heats up in Atlanta, White Water has lots of ways for you to cool off. For heart-thumping thrills, the **100-Meter Splash** sends you plummeting headfirst down a 365-foot slide in a race against five other sliders.

You can jump waves, or ride them on colorful inner tubes, at the **Atlanta Ocean**, a giant wave pool. **Little Hooch** is a miniature version of the Chattahoochee River where you can paddle or drift gently downstream. Your whole family can ride down the massive **Bahama Bob-Slide**. It's over two football fields long. Ride down the **Bermuda Triangle** or **Black River Falls** for more watery fun.

There are rafts big enough for the whole family at White Water.

You can walk on water in the Activity Pool. Colorful disks, like rocks in a stream, are placed across the pool. You can hop from one to another.

The Bahama Bob-Slide

SUPER SLIDERS

These kids slid down the water slides and left their towels behind. By tracing each slider back to where he or she started, can you discover who each towel belongs to?

AMERICAN ADVENTURES

This is the place for riding and sliding, bumping and heart-thumping family fun. This park is filled with indoor and outdoor entertainment that will keep you happy for hours! You'll find amusement rides like go-carts and a ship that swings way up high. You can also play in the arcade or try a round of miniature golf.

The Galleon swings riders high in the air.

The **Foam Factory** is a zany multi-level fun house unlike anything you've ever seen before. It's filled with foam balls that are launched at you in dozens of ways. You can see the giant foam art and plan your own do-it-yourself inventions. There's even a foam-ball roller coaster!

The Foam Factory is a foam fun house.

WHAT'S WRONG HERE?

Circle 16 things you think are wrong with this picture. When you're done, color the scene.

CNN CENTER

You've seen them on TV, now you can see broadcast journalists in action. The Atlanta headquarters of CNN and *Headline News* is located at CNN Center. You can join one of the regularly scheduled tours to get an inside look at the amazing technology it takes to put out the news 24 hours a day. You'll view the newsroom from a special route that lets you see the entire scene laid out below. Through the glass you can watch the flurry of activity as the journalists, editors, producers, and technicians prepare and deliver the news live on the air.

The bustling news floor at CNN

CNN Center

The Turner Store at CNN Center is packed with souvenirs and movie items.

DON'T SNOOZE THROUGH THE NEWS

Without telling anyone what you're doing, ask for a word to fill in each blank. For example, "Give me an action word." When all the blanks are filled in, read the story out loud. One of the blanks has been filled in for you.

Julee and ____________ (boy's name 1) were on their ____________ (number) day at Channel 1 News. "Our show is too slow (describing word)," said the station manager. "It's putting people to sleep. Fix it or you're fired!" The he ________ (action word)ed out of the ____________ (place). "____________ (exclamation)" groaned ____________ (boy's name 1). "What are we going to do?" "I've got an idea," Julee said ________ (emotion)ly. That night when it was time for the news, a ____________ (describing word) band ____________ (action word)ed in front of the camera. "Don't snooze through the news!" they shouted. They played their ____________ (things) loudly as they ____________ (action word)ed off stage.

SIX FLAGS OVER GEORGIA

Here you'll find all the wild and crazy excitement you could want, with entertainment and over 100 rides.

Five of the world's scariest roller coasters are here: the Great American Scream Machine, Georgia Cyclone, Mine Train, Viper, NINJA, and Mind Bender. On hot summer days you'll enjoy making a big splash with some of the South's wildest and wettest water adventures: Thunder River, Splashwater Falls, Raging Rivers, and the Log Flume.

⇑ Kids talking to a "furry friend" at Bugs Bunny World

Bugs Bunny World is a special area full of rides and attractions for younger thrill seekers. Kids can even eat with Bugs Bunny and his *Looney Tunes* friends at the Carrot Club.

The whole family will enjoy an old-fashioned sing-along with live music at the **Crystal Pistol Music Hall** or the **Remember When Drive-in.**

Soar through the skies on Free Fall — the ride that's like falling off a 10-story building

⇑ The roller coaster at Six Flags

MIXED-UP PICTURE STORY

To find out what's happening at the amusement park, put the scene in the correct order by filling in the number box in the bottom corner of each picture. When you're done, color in the scene.

ATLANTA CYCLORAMA

The world's largest painting, at the Cyclorama

Cannons blast and soldiers shout—you're right in the middle of the Battle of Atlanta on July 22, 1864. This event is re-created through the three-dimensional painting that surrounds you at the Atlanta Cyclorama. The story of the battle is told with lights and music as the auditorium revolves to reveal different aspects of the entire event.

The 9,000-pound painting is considered the world's largest. At 358 x 42 feet it's longer than a football field and taller than a 5-story building. European artists painted the scene with amazing detail. It includes landscaping, wagons, railroad ties, and 128 soldiers carefully sculpted into the front of the scene to blend with the painting.

The Cyclorama building also contains a museum where you can view uniforms, weapons, and other Civil War items. The huge steam locomotive *Texas* takes up a large area of the first floor. It played a starring role in the great locomotive chase of April 1862 when the Confederates ran it backward to catch another locomotive stolen by the Union Army.

COLOR TO FIND THE ANSWER

You can see one of these at the Atlanta Cyclorama. Color the shapes with 1 dot red. Color the shapes with 2 dots gray, and color the shapes with four dots black. Color the other shapes any colors you want.

BABYLAND GENERAL HOSPITAL

Cabbage Patch Kids

Doll hugs are delivered at the Babyland General Hospital. It was built as an actual medical clinic several decades ago, but now Cabbage Patch Kids are born here.

The fun starts when you walk in and your LPN (Licensed "Patch" Nurse) welcomes you in the Fathers' Waiting Room. You can visit the hospital, talk to the doctors and nurses, and see the babies in their cribs. Watch as the dolls are delivered from the mother cabbages and help name the new babies. You can greet the Cabbage Patch Kids in the school-room, by the wishing pond, or under the Magic Crystal Tree.

Be sure to see the display of early soft-sculpture dolls. Originally known as Little People, some dolls are now worth over $10,000!

Babyland General Hospital is located in Cleveland, Georgia, a little over an hour's drive north of Atlanta, but if you're a doll collector (or just a doll lover) it's one hospital you won't want to miss.

MY TRAVEL JOURNAL

—That's Entertainment—

These are the names of the places I visited: ______________________________

My favorite place was: ______________________________

The strangest thing I saw was: ______________________________

This is a picture of something I saw

8 LET'S EAT!

The Varsity serves hotdogs and other American favorites.

PEOPLE IN ATLANTA LOVE TO EAT OUT. From down-home Southern cooking to exotic dishes from around the world, Atlanta has more restaurants than you can begin to imagine.

For something casual, try a Georgia barbecue or take a picnic to a park. Lots of places, from fast-food to fancy restaurants, will provide food to go.

For something different, try one of Atlanta's many ethnic restaurants. Enjoy the tastes of China, Cuba, France, India, Korea, Mexico, Vietnam, and many other countries.

If you just want a quick snack, you'll find lots of food courts at the major malls. Special shops sell pastries, candy, and ice cream. When you visit Atlanta, prepare your taste buds for treats!

Downtown Atlanta Dining

1. Alon's at the Terrace
2. Alon's Bakery
3. Gorin's
4. Hard Rock Café
5. Planet Hollywood
6. Silver Skillet
7. Touch of India

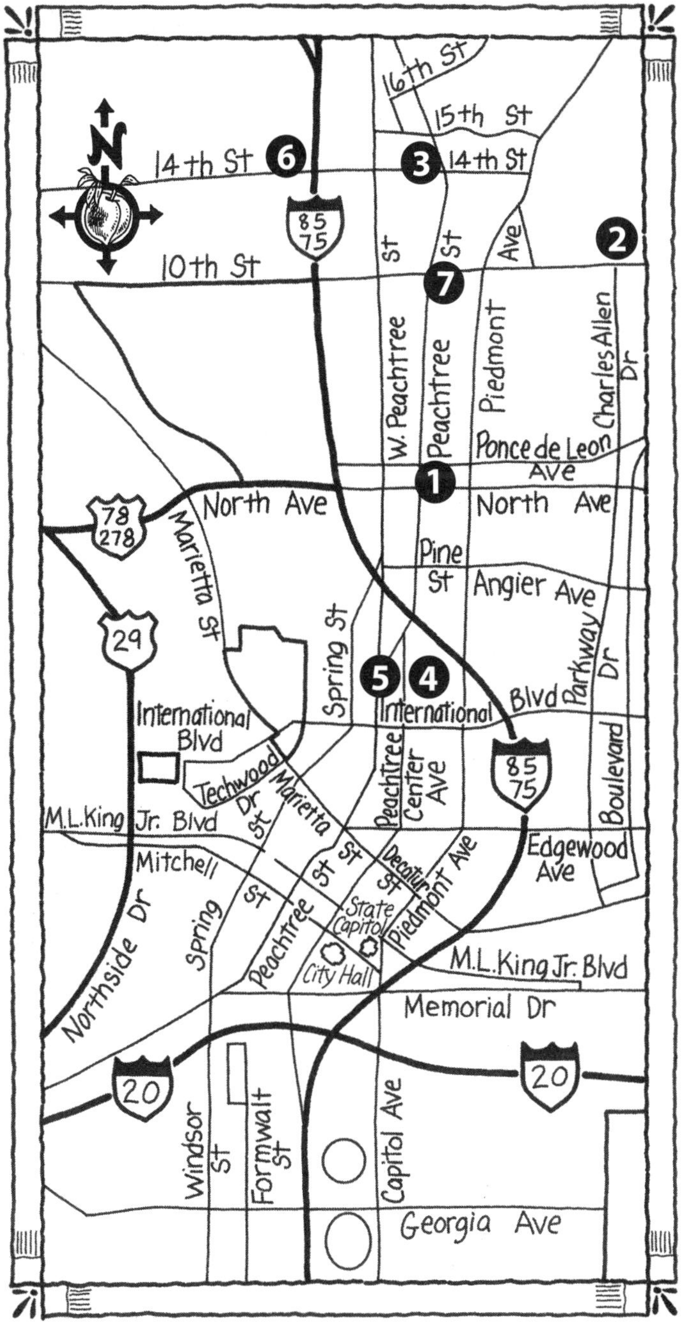

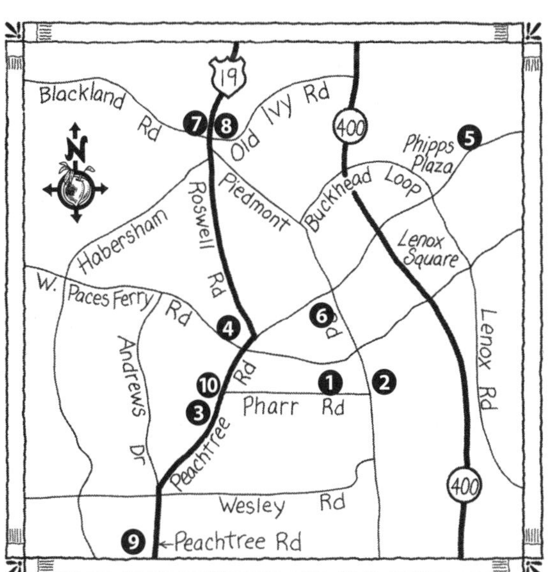

Buckhead Dining

1. Buckhead Bread Co.
2. Buckhead Diner
3. Cheesecake Factory
4. Johnny Rockets
5. Johnny Rockets (in Phipps)
6. Kudzu Café
7. La Fonda Latina
8. Landmark Diner
9. Rocky's Brick Oven Pizza
10. Three Dollar Café

BEST BARBECUES

There are lots of different ways to make barbecue sauce and everyone thinks his or her recipe is the best. One way to try them all at once is at **Spring Fest**, which is held at Stone Mountain Park each May. You can wander from grill to grill tasting barbecue ribs, pork, and chicken wings.

Rib Ranch

There are many good barbecue restaurants in Atlanta. **Bobby and June's Country Kitchen** has an old-time Southern feeling that's perfect for trying barbecue and real Southern biscuits. The restaurant still uses the original barbecue pit with hickory wood for a traditional flavor. While you eat, check out the old farm tools on the walls, pictures of houses from the 1900s, and original Atlanta street signs.

The **Rib Ranch**, in the Buckhead district, serves Texas-style barbecue, some made right in the Ranch's smokehouse.

Leftovers never tasted so good. Brunswick stew is a delicious combo of leftover chunks of barbecued meat and corn, tomatoes, and spices.

Spring Fest at Stone Mountain Park

HIDE AND SEEK!

Draw circles around the hidden objects in this drawing of a barbecue at Stone Mountain Park.
Hint: There are 15 objects.
When you're done, color the scene.

SOUTHERN FAVORITES

The Southern breakfast is a delicious meal of scrambled eggs, bacon or ham, grits, fried apples, and, of course, biscuits. Biscuits should be light and flaky, tender, and hot so the butter melts.

For a traditional Southern breakfast, try the **Silver Skillet** on 14th Street, at this location since 1956. It's not fancy, but it is authentic. In fact, it's even been featured in movies and commercials. You can eat breakfast here all day long, or try one of the other specialties that are offered at very reasonable prices.

The Silver Skillet, an authentic diner

At the **Southern Skillet** in Roswell, the walls are packed with souvenirs from this historic city, and the food is true Southern style.

The **Kudzu Café** is named and decorated after the fast-growing vine that's taking over the South. From brunch through dinner, you can choose from pasta, salads, vegetable plates, and even Kudzu Ice Cream Moon Pie!

Grits are small flakes of corn that are hulled and dried, then cooked in water. Top them with butter or cheese.

UNSCRAMBLE THE FOODS

dfier pelaps

tgsri

stbuciis

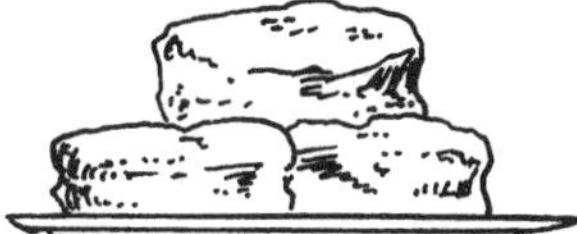

irfed ncikehc

nomo epi

In this activity, unscramble each word and match it to the Southern food it describes.

ETHNIC FOODS

Rio Bravo Cantina

What kind of food do you like? If you like to try different kinds of food, you'll have lots of choices in Atlanta's ethnic restaurants.

You'll probably like the chips, tacos, and burritos served at a variety of Mexican restaurants. With several locations, **Rio Bravo Cantina** and **El Azteca**—which occasionally has mariachi singers—are sure to please.

La Fonda Latina is a Cuban eatery with atmosphere. Just look for the giant painted banana trees and zigzag roof in blue, purple, and green. Try *paella*, a specialty that includes rice, shrimp, chicken, sausage, and peppers.

At **Touch of India** you can order a variety of traditional Indian dishes. It's fun to try several by sharing with others at the table.

Other choices range from A to V—from Australian to Vietnamese. In between you can try Ethiopian, French, German, Greek, Thai, and so many others we can't name them all here. Be adventurous and try something new!

ATLANTA'S FAVORITE FOODS

Hidden in this word search are some of the foods you might try in Atlanta. Search for words vertically, horizontally, and diagonally. Can you find all 10 words? The first word has been found for you.

Word Box

grits	moon pie
barbecue ribs	chicken wings
cornbread	biscuits
eclairs	cheesecake
pizza	ice cream

W B I S C U I T S T P M S P V U H
P A Y F V D Q J O X P B B D Y E H
O I C H I C K E N W I N G S L C X
G T P O D Y W K X R P A T U M L N
O G Y R G S I C E C R E A M O A N
H R P A M U F U G N B O E T O I Y
Y I S I L U C N H T R U V E N R P
P T X C H E E S E C A K E R P S W
I S T D B X R O M B O A G F I Q T
Z A R R P S A R L P Y J N L E O B
Z O A B L M A T E I L O M F N F W
A B Q B C O R N B R E A D E T Q R

THE NEWEST OLD-STYLE DINERS

Family diners serve good food in large portions, and Atlanta has some unforgettable ones.

Johnny Rockets looks just like an old-time soda fountain with gleaming stainless steel, glass, and old-fashioned counter stools and booths. You'll love the thick, juicy burgers and fries, but save room for a fabulous thick malt or milk shake.

The **Landmark Diner** is the largest diner, and it's open 24 hours a day, seven days a week. Breads and pastries are baked from scratch daily. It serves all-American favorites plus delicious Greek specialties. No one leaves hungry.

The **Buckhead Diner** is a fancy diner decorated with chrome, glass, and neon. The food is more sophisticated than at most diners, and the combinations of ingredients are delicious.

Buckhead Diner

Johnny Rockets

WHAT'S THE DIFFERENCE?

These two pictures of a family at an Atlanta diner might look the same, but they are not. How many differences between the two scenes can you find? Hint: There are at least 15 differences.

BRING ON THE GLITZ!

Discover California and London on Peachtree Street at two glamorous restaurants in downtown Atlanta.

At **Planet Hollywood**, you might get sidetracked before you order your meal. You'll be too busy trying to see all the movie items on your favorite stars, like the rotating life-size model of Arnold Schwarzenegger as the Terminator. Along the wall outside you can match your hand prints to those of the stars—Cher, Billy Crystal, Paul Newman, Kevin Costner, Roseanne . . . Who else can you find?

The **Hard Rock Café** is filled with the pulsing beat of—what else?—rock 'n' roll. It's packed with hundreds of items relating to Michael Jackson, the Beatles, Elvis, Madonna, and many other famous recording artists. Favorite foods on the menu include "Love Me Tender" chicken fingers, burgers, and nachos.

Dine with the stars at Planet Hollywood.

The original Hard Rock Café was created in London, England. Two Americans living there decided that Europeans should have a taste of American food with rock 'n' roll flavor.

Hard Rock Café

WHICH ARE THE SAME?

Two of the peaches in this bunch are twins.
Circle the two that are exactly the same.

DELICIOUS DESSERTS

For chocolate eclairs that melt in your mouth—and tons of other delicious, fresh-baked goodies—visit **Alon's at the Terrace** across from the Fox Theatre or the **Alon's Bakery** in the Virginia Highlands area.

At the **Buckhead Bread Company** you can choose from shelf upon shelf of rich pastries, or try gelato, creamy Italian ice cream. This is a good spot to have lunch. The sandwiches are made on fresh breads that are as good as the desserts.

The **Cheesecake Factory** is famous for its rich, creamy cheesecake. You can pick a traditional version or choose from more than 30 exotic flavors like Chocolate Peanut Butter, Crazy Carrot Cake, or Oreo Cheesecake.

On a "Hotlanta" day, ice cream tastes terrific. Try **Gorin's Homemade Café & Grill**, with locations near many of Atlanta's most popular shopping and entertainment sites. The ice cream is homemade and so are the special grilled sandwiches. Or find a **Ben & Jerry's** ice cream store (the airport has two locations!).

Tasty choices at the Cheesecake Factory

WHAT'S IN COMMON?

Each of these desserts has something in common with the other two in the same row. For example, all of the desserts in the the top row are pieces of pie. Draw a line through each row and describe what the desserts in that row have in common. Don't forget to include diagonals!

FINGER FOODS

The **Varsity**, Atlanta's traditional "greasy spoon diner," has been serving Georgia Tech students since 1928. The Varsity now has a few other restaurants in the suburbs and in Athens, but try to visit the original. Sit at one of the school-style desks and gobble the greasy food surrounded by the noise of conversation and TVs.

If you like pizza, there are plenty of restaurants to choose from. The best pizza place to visit is **Rocky's Brick Oven Pizza**. You can make your own pizza in the kitchen—toss the dough yourself and spread on the sauce and cheese. Be sure to look at the wall of photos signed by famous people like Jimmy Carter and Toni Braxton.

Rocky's has even starred in a children's book, *Rocky Bobocky, The Pizza Man.*

The **Three Dollar Café** is known for the best chicken wings in Atlanta. Choose yours hot, medium, or mild. There's also a wide range of other finger foods here.

The Varsity, an Atlanta tradition

MY TRAVEL JOURNAL

—Let's Eat!—

These are the names of some of the restaurants I ate at:

____

My favorite restaurant was: ______________________________

The most unusual food I ate was: ______________________________

My least favorite food was: ______________________________

This is a picture of one restaurant I visited

CALENDAR OF ATLANTA EVENTS

There's always something fun to do in Atlanta. But during certain times of the year, you'll discover special events. Whatever month you visit, check the list below and see if there's something you'd like to attend.

January

King Week

Martin Luther King Jr. Center, (404) 524-1956
This annual celebration honors the birthday (January 15) and accomplishments of Dr. Martin Luther King Jr.

Peach Bowl

Georgia Dome, (404) 586-8500
Enjoy the football game and a downtown parade with floats and marching bands.

February

Groundhog Day

Yellow River Game Ranch, (770) 972-6643
Visit General Lee the groundhog to find out if he sees his shadow.

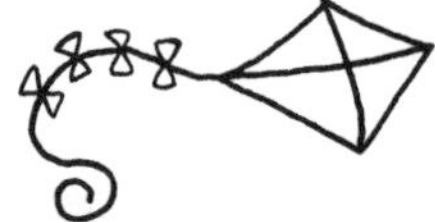

March

Atlanta 500

Atlanta Motor Speedway, (770) 946-4211
A NASCAR event, this professional stock-car race is part of the Winston Cup Series.

April

Dogwood Festival

Piedmont Park, (404) 329-0501
Celebrate spring with flowering dogwoods. Events include parades, home and garden tours, art shows, and musical entertainment.

Kids Fishing Event

Sponsored by the Georgia Department of Natural Resources, (770) 781-6888
Your odds of catching "the big one" go up when the Chattahoochee River is stocked with over 2,500 trout for this event.

Georgia Renaissance Festival

Fairburn, (770) 964-8575
Every weekend from late April through June (also October and November). An old English village comes to life with games, entertainment, food, music, and historical characters.

May

Music Midtown

(404) 872-1115
This three-day festival will get your feet tapping to the beat with music that includes rock, alternative, R & B, gospel, jazz, folk, reggae, and children's songs.

Atlanta Jazz Festival

Woodruff Park and Grand Park, (404) 817-6815
National and international jazz musicians perform.

June

DeKalb International Choral Festival

Various locations throughout the Atlanta metropolitan area, (404) 378-2525
Choruses from the United States and around the world perform.

Hispanic Festival of Music and the Arts

(770) 938-8611
Hear Spanish and Latin music reflecting a variety of countries influenced by Hispanic culture.

Willie B's Birthday Party

Zoo Atlanta, (404) 624-5808
The silverback gorilla gets a giant birthday cake. Kids share the fun with cake, face painting, music, and other activities.

Civil War Encampment

Atlanta History Center, (404) 814-4000
See what life was like in a tent on a Civil War battlefield. Music, food, and other exhibitions.

July

Fantastic Fourth of July Celebration

Stone Mountain Park, (770) 498-5702
A music concert, laser show, and a fabulous fireworks display that lights up the mountain.

Independence Day Celebration

Lenox Square, (404) 233-6767
Bring lawn chairs and blankets to see one of the largest and most spectacular annual fireworks shows in the Southeast.

Peachtree Road Race

Lenox Square to Piedmont Park, (404) 231-9065
Cheer for 50,000 runners from all over the world during the 10-kilometer race on July 4.

August

Marietta Art in the Park

Marietta Square, (770) 528-0616
See original paintings, pottery, photography, and other media at this three-day display of fine arts.

September

Arts Festival of Atlanta

Downtown, (404) 885-1125
A huge outdoor art fair with paintings, prints, jewelry, crafts, handmade toys, lots of food, entertainment, and much more.

Folklife Festival

Atlanta History Center, (404) 814-4000
This event re-creates farming life in North Georgia in the 1840s. See period crafts such as candle and soap making, and weaving.

Gwinnett County Fair

Gwinnett, (770) 963-6522
One of the largest fairs in Georgia, including livestock competitions, entertainment, beauty contests, and fireworks.

Yellow Daisy Festival

Stone Mountain Park, (770) 498-5702
See traditional country crafts from over 500 exhibitors at one of the largest outdoor festivals in the Southeast.

October

Atlanta Greek Festival

Cathedral of the Annunciation, (404) 633-5870
Pretend you're in the Greek Isles with live entertainment and authentic Greek food.

Great Miller Lite Chili Cookoff

Stone Mountain Park, (770) 498-5702
Taste chili and Brunswick stew created by cooks who compete each year.

Tour of Southern Ghosts

Stone Mountain Park, (770) 498-5702
Enjoy storytelling and other kids' activities to celebrate Halloween.

Rhoades Hall Haunted House

Midtown, (404) 881-9980
Get spooked at an historic home that's been converted into a scare factory!

Jonesboro Fall Festival and Battle Reenactment

Jonesboro, (770) 473-0197
See 500 authentically uniformed soldiers re-enacting the Battle of Jonesboro. Live entertainment, antiques, arts and crafts, and tours of the mid-1800s Stately Oaks Plantation.

Stone Mountain Scottish Highland Games

Stone Mountain, (404) 498-5702
Traditional Scottish activities such as caber toss and dancing, plus food and fantastic fife-and-drum and military brass band performances.

November

Lighting of the Great Tree

Underground Atlanta, (404) 523-2311
At night, see the huge Christmas tree lit up in this traditional Thanksgiving event.

December

Festival of Trees

Downtown, (404) 264-9348
Enjoy the train rides, a carousel, parade, and fabulous displays of holiday decorations. Benefit event for the, Egleston Children's Hospital

Zoo Atlanta's Breakfast and Supper with Santa

Zoo Atlanta, (404) 624-5600
Santa Claus joins young guests for either breakfast or supper.

Candlelight Tours

Atlanta History Center, (404) 814-4000
Re-creates traditional holiday celebrations of the 1920s and 1930s at the Swan House and a holiday celebration from the early nineteenth century at Tullie Smith House.

First Night

Several Midtown blocks, (404) 881-0400
Celebrate New Year's Eve at this non-alcoholic event for the entire family featuring live music, puppet performances, theater, and other activities.

RESOURCE GUIDE: WHEN, WHAT, AND HOW MUCH?

Below are addresses and information on Atlanta sights that you may find interesting. We've included phone numbers to make it easy to call for more information. Check with the specific sight before visiting because the days and hours of operation, as well as the admissions fee, may change.

If You Get Lost

Make a plan with your parents in case you become separated. For example, if you're in a store, you could go to a person working at a cash register. If you're outside, you could look for a mother with children and tell her you're lost.

In an emergency, you can easily call the police, fire department, or an ambulance from any phone. You won't need coins. Just dial 911.

Emergency Numbers

Injury, accident, fire, or emergency 911
Poison Control (404) 616-9000
Ambulance 911
Atlanta South Ambulance Service, Inc.
(404) 763-8888
MEDSTAT Emergency Medical Service, Inc.
(404) 361-2273

Medical and Dental Services

Crawford Long Hospital of Emory University
(404) 686-4411
Emory Health Connection Physician Referral
(404) 778-7744
Georgia Dental Association (referrals)
(404) 636-7553
Medical Association of Atlanta (referrals)
(404) 881-1714
Pharmacy (24-hour) (404) 876-0381

Transportation

Public Transit

Cobb Community Transit (CCT) (770) 427-4444
MARTA (Metro Atlanta Rapid Transit Authority)
(404) 848-4711

Car Travel and Rentals

AAA Auto Club South (404) 724-2110
Alamo Rent-A-Car (404) 768-4161
Avis Rent-A-Car (404) 530-2700
Dollar Rent-A-Car (404) 766-0244
Hertz Car Rental (404) 530-2900
National Car Rental (404) 530-2800
Thrifty Car Rental (404) 524-2843

Bus

Greyhound Bus Terminal (800) 231-2222

Taxis

Atlanta Royal (404) 584-6655
Buckhead Safety (404) 233-1152
Checker Cab Company (404) 351-1111
University Yellow Cab (404) 521-0200

Train

Southern Railways–Amtrak (800) 872-7245

Tourist Information

Atlanta Convention and Visitors Bureau (404) 222-6688

Cobb County Convention and Visitors Bureau (770) 933-7228

DeKalb Convention and Visitors Bureau (404) 378-2525

Georgia Council for International Visitors (404) 240-0042

Gwinnett Convention and Visitors Bureau (770) 931-6960

What They Cost and When They're Open

African American Panoramic Experience (APEX), 135 Auburn Avenue. Open Tuesday through Saturday from 10 a.m. to 5 p.m. throughout the year, Sunday from 1 p.m. to 5 p.m. during summer. Admission is $3 for adults, $2 for students and seniors, free for children under 4. (404) 521-2739

Alon's at the Terrace, 659 Peachtree Road. Open Monday from 11 a.m. to 2:30 p.m. (to 8 p.m. for Fox Theatre performances), Tuesday through Thursday from 11 a.m. to 11 p.m., Friday and Saturday from 11 a.m. to midnight. Closed Sunday (except during Fox Theatre performances, open 11 a.m. to 8 p.m.). (404) 724-0444

Alon's Bakery, 1394 N. Highland Ave. Open seven days from 7 a.m. to 7 p.m. (404) 872-6000

American Adventures, 250 N. Cobb Parkway, Marietta. Open seasonally in summer, Sunday through Friday from 11 a.m. to 9 p.m., Saturday from 10 a.m. to 10 p.m. Admission for all rides $3 for a parent pass, $15 for children, $5 for children under 2. (770) 424-9283

Atlanta Botanical Garden, 1345 Piedmont Avenue N.E. Open Tuesday through Sunday from 9 a.m. to 6 p.m. Admission is $6 for adults, $3 for students (elementary through college), free for children 5 and under. (404) 876-5859

Atlanta Botanical Garden

Atlanta Cyclorama, 800 Cherokee Avenue S.E., (Grant Park). Open the Tuesday after Labor Day through May 31st from 9:20 a.m. to 4:30 p.m., June through Labor Day from 9:20 a.m. to 5:30 p.m. Admission $5 for adults, $4 for senior citizens, $3 for children ages 6 to 12, free for children under 6. (404) 658-7625

Atlanta Heritage Row, 55 Upper Alabama Street (Underground Atlanta). Open Tuesday through Saturday from 10 a.m. to 5 p.m., Sunday from 1 p.m. to 5 p.m. Admission $3 for adults, $2 for students and seniors, free for children under 6. (404) 584-7879

Atlanta History Center, 130 West Paces Ferry Road. Open Monday through Saturday from 10 a.m. to 5:30 p.m., Sunday from 12 noon to 5:30 p.m. Admission $7 for adults, $5 for students 18 and up or seniors 65 and up, $4 for children ages 6 to 17, free for children under 5. Tours of the historic houses are an additional $1 each. (404) 814-4000

Atlanta International Museum of Art and Design, 285 Peachtree Center Avenue (Peachtree Center, Marquis Two Tower). Open Tuesday through Saturday from 11 a.m. to 5 p.m. Admission by donation. (404) 688-2467

Atlanta Motor Speedway, 1500 U.S. Highways 19 and 41 S., Hampton. Open for tours Monday through Friday from 9 a.m. to 5 p.m., Saturday from 9 a.m. to 4:30 p.m., Sunday from 1 p.m. to 4:30 p.m. No tours during race weeks. Tour admission $3. (770) 707-7970

Babyland General Hospital, 73 West Underwood Street, Cleveland. Open Monday through Saturday from 9 a.m. to 5 p.m., Sunday from 10 a.m. to 5 p.m. Admission free. (706) 865-2171

BellSouth Pioneer Museum, 675 W. Peachtree Street N.E. Open Monday through Friday from 11 a.m. to 1 p.m. Admission free. (404) 529-0971

Ben and Jerry's, 1425 Market Boulevard, Suite 300, Roswell, (770) 992-8168; Concourse A and C, Hartsfield International Airport, (404) 767-5086; 5920 Roswell Road, (404) 255-3528.

Big Shanty Museum, 2829 Cherokee Street, Kennesaw. Open Monday through Saturday from 9:30 a.m. to 5:30 p.m., Sunday from 12:30 p.m. to 5:30 p.m. Admission $3 for adults, $2.50 for seniors, $1.50 for children ages 7 to 15, free for children under 7. (770) 427-2117

Bobby and June's Country Kitchen, 375 14th Street N.W. Open Monday through Friday from 6 a.m. to 8 p.m., Saturday 6 a.m. to 2 p.m. Closed Sunday. (404) 876-3872

Buckhead Bread Company, 3070 Piedmont Road. Open Sunday through Thursday from 6:30 a.m. to 8 p.m., Friday and Saturday from 6:30 a.m. to 9 p.m. (404) 240-1978

Buckhead Diner, 3073 Piedmont Road. Open Monday through Saturday from 10:45 a.m. to midnight, Sunday from 10 a.m. to 10 p.m. (404) 262-3336

Bulloch Hall, 180 Bulloch Avenue, Roswell. Open Monday through Saturday from 10 a.m. to 2 p.m., Sunday from 1 p.m. to 3 p.m. All tours on the hour. Admission $5 for adults, $3 for children ages 6 to 16, free for children 5 and under. (770) 992-1731

Callaway Gardens, Highway 27, Pine Mountain. Open daylight to dark (7 a.m. to 7 p.m. summer,

8 a.m. to 5 p.m. winter). Admission $20 per vehicle spring and summer, $15 per vehicle fall and winter. (800) 282-8181

Carter Presidential Center, 441 Freedom Parkway. Open Monday through Saturday from 9 a.m. to 4:45 p.m., Sunday from 12 noon to 4:45 p.m. Admission $6 for adults, $5 for seniors 55 and up, free for children under 16. (404) 331-0296

Center for Puppetry Arts, 1404 Spring Street. Open Monday through Saturday from 9 a.m. to 5 p.m. Admission $5 for adults, $2 for children. Special events additional cost. (404) 873-3391

A puppeteer working behind the scenes at the Center for Puppetry Arts

Chattahoochee Nature Center, 9135 Willeo Road, Roswell. Open Monday through Saturday from 9 a.m. to 5 p.m., Sunday from 12 noon to 5 p.m. Admission $2 for adults, $1 for children and senior citizens, free for children under 3. (770) 992-2055

Chattahoochee Outdoor Center, 1990 Island Ford Parkway. Open weekdays from 10 a.m. to 8 p.m., Saturday and Sunday from 9 a.m. to 8 p.m. Canoe and raft rentals from $35 to $80. (770) 395-6851

Cheesecake Factory, 3024 Peachtree Road N.W. Open Monday through Thursday from 11:30 a.m. to 12:30 p.m., Friday and Saturday from 11:30 a.m. to 1:30 a.m., Sunday from 10 a.m. to 12 midnight. (404) 816-2555

CNN Center, One CNN Center, at Techwood Drive and Marietta Street. Open Monday through Sunday from 9:00 a.m. to 6:00 p.m. Tour admission $7 for adults, $5 for seniors 65 and older, $4.50 for children 12 and under. Tour not recommended for children under 6. (404) 827-1500

El Azteca restaurants, 6078 Roswell Road, (404) 255-9807; 939 Ponce de Leon Avenue N.E., (404) 881-6040; 5800 Buford Highway, (770) 452-7192; 6100 Roswell Road N.W., (404) 256-9930; 25 Auburn Avenue, (404) 521-2584; 3424 Piedmont Road, (404) 266-3787; 880 Atlanta Street, Roswell, (770) 998-6553; 135 S. Main Street, Alpharetta, (770) 664-4868; 9926 Haynes Bridge Road, Alpharetta, (770) 569-5234.

Federal Reserve Bank Monetary Museum, 104 Marietta Street N.W. Open Monday through Friday from 9 a.m. to 4:30 p.m. Admission free. (404) 521-8764

Fernbank Museum of Natural History, 767 Clifton Road. Open Monday through Saturday from 10 a.m. to 5 p.m., Sunday from noon to 5 p.m. Museum admission $9.50 for adults, $8 for students over 12 and seniors, $7 for children ages 3 to 12, free for children under 3. IMAX combination tickets are $14.50 for adults, $12 for students and seniors, $10 for children ages 3 to 12. (404) 378-0127

Fernbank Science Center, 156 Heaton Park Drive N.E. Open Monday from 8:30 a.m. to 5 p.m., Tuesday through Friday from 8:30 a.m. to 10 p.m., Saturday from 10 a.m. to 5 p.m., Sunday from 1 p.m. to 5 p.m. Science Center admission free. Planetarium admission $2 for adults, $1 for children 5 and up. Admission for children's shows $.50. (404) 378-4311

Fox Theatre, 660 Peachtree Street N.E. Tours held on Monday, Wednesday, and Thursday at 10:00 a.m., Saturday at 10:00 a.m. and 11:00 a.m. Admission $5 for adults, $4 for seniors, $3 for students. (404) 881-2100

Georgia Dome, 1 Georgia Dome Drive. Open Tuesday through Saturday from 10 a.m. to 4 p.m., Sunday noon to 4 p.m. All tours on the hour. Admission $4 for adults, $2.50 for seniors and children ages 5 to 12, free for children under 5. (404) 223-9200

Georgia State Capitol, Capitol and Washington Streets. Open Monday through Friday from 8 a.m. to 5 p.m., Saturday from 10 a.m. to 4 p.m., Sunday from noon to 4 p.m. Admission free. (404) 656-2844

Georgia State Museum of Science and Industry, Capitol Hill and Washington Streets. Open Monday through Friday from 8 a.m. to 5 p.m., Saturday from 10 a.m. to 4 p.m., Sunday from 12 noon to 4 p.m. Admission free. (404) 656-2844

Gorin's Homemade Café & Grill, 1170 Peachtree Street, (404) 892-2500; 620 Peachtree Street, (404) 874-0550; Phipps Plaza, (404) 231-5244; 1228 West Paces Ferry Road, (404) 266-3349; Peachtree Center, (404) 521-9266; CNN Center, (404) 521-0588; 1155 Mount Vernon Highway.

Governor's Mansion, 391 West Paces Ferry Road. Open Tuesday, Wednesday, and Thursday, tours from 10 a.m. to 11:30 a.m. Admission free. (404) 261-1776

Hard Rock Café, 215 Peachtree Street N.E. Open daily from 11 a.m. to 2 a.m. (404) 688-7625

High Museum of Art, 1280 Peachtree Street N.E. Open Tuesday through Saturday from 10 a.m. to 5 p.m., Sunday from 12 noon to 5 p.m. Admission $6 for adults, $4 for students and seniors, $2 for children ages 6 to 17, free for children under 6. Admission free Thursdays from 1 p.m. to 5 p.m. Special exhibitions may have a surcharge. (404) 733-4444

High Museum of Art, Folk Art & Photography Galleries, 30 John Wesley Dobbs Avenue N.E. Open Monday through Saturday from 10 a.m. to 5 p.m. Admission $5 for adults, $4 for seniors and college students, $3 for children, free for residents of Fulton County or High Museum members. (404) 577-6940

Johnny Rockets

Johnny Rockets, 5 West Paces Ferry Road, Buckhead, (404) 231-5555; 6510 Roswell Road, Sandy Springs, (404) 257-0677; Phipps Plaza, (404) 233-9867; 2970 Cobb Parkway, (770) 955-6068; Underground Atlanta, (404) 525-7117. Open Sunday through Thursday from 11 a.m. to 10:30 p.m., Friday and Saturday until 2 a.m.

Kennesaw Mountain National Battlefield Park, 900 Kennesaw Mountain Drive, Kennesaw. Open daily from 8:30 a.m. to 5 p.m. Admission free. (770) 427-4686

Kudzu Café, 3215 Peachtree Road. Open Sunday through Thursday from 11 a.m. to 11 p.m., Friday and Saturday from 11 a.m. to midnight. (404) 262-0661

La Fonda Latina, 2813 Peachtree Road N.E., Buckhead, (404) 816-8311; 4427 Roswell Road N.E., (404) 303-8201; 1150 B. Euclid Avenue (Little Five Points), (404) 577-8317; 1639 McLendon Avenue, (404) 378-5200. Open Sunday through Thursday from 11:30 a.m. to 11 p.m., Friday and Saturday from 11:30 a.m. to midnight.

Lake Lanier Islands, 6950 Holiday Road, Lake Lanier Islands. Islands open year round. Admission at entrance gate $5 per car. Admission $15 for adults and children over 42 inches tall, $8 for children under 42 inches tall, $8 for seniors 60 or older. (770) 932-7200

Landmark Diner, 3652 Roswell Road N.E. Open 24 hours, seven days a week. (404) 816-9090

Martin Luther King Jr. Historical Site, 449 Auburn Avenue N.E. Open daily from 9 a.m. to 5 p.m. Admission free. (404) 524-1956

Michael C. Carlos Museum, Emory University Quadrangle, 571 South Kilgo Street. Open Monday through Saturday from 10 a.m. to 5 p.m., Sunday from 12 noon to 5 p.m. Admission $3 suggested donation. (404) 727-4282

Mountasia Family Fun Centers, 1099 Johnson Ferry Road, Marietta, (770) 977-1200; 175 Ernest Barrett Parkway, Marietta; (770) 422-3440; 8510 Holcomb Bridge Road, (770) 993-7711. Open Monday through Thursday from 10 a.m. to 11 p.m., Friday and Saturday from 10 a.m. to midnight, Sunday from 10 a.m. to 11 p.m. Admission free, but fees for activities. Golf $5.70 for adults, $4.50 for children. Bumper boat or go-carts are $3.50.

Museum of Atlanta History, see Atlanta History Center.

Oakland Cemetery, 248 Oakland Avenue S.E. Grounds open spring and summer daily from 8 a.m. to 7 p.m., fall and winter from 8 a.m. to 6 p.m. Visitor Center open Monday through Friday from 9 a.m. to 5 p.m. Admission free. (404) 658-6019

Omni Sports Coliseum, 100 Techwood Drive, (404) 681-2100

Planet Hollywood, 218 Peachtree Street. Open daily from 11 a.m. to 1 a.m. (404) 523-7300

Rib Ranch, 25 Irby Avenue. Open Monday through Saturday from 11 a.m. to 11 p.m., Sunday from 12 noon to 10 p.m. (404) 233-7644

Road to Tara Museum, 659 Peachtree Street (The Georgian Terrace). Open Monday through Saturday from 10 a.m. to 6 p.m., Sunday from 1 p.m. to 6 p.m. Admission $6 for adults, $4 for students, $4.50 for seniors, free for children under 8. (404) 897-1939

Rocky's Brick Oven Pizza, 1770 Peachtree Street N.W. Open Monday through Thursday from 11:30 a.m. to 11 p.m., Friday from 11:30 a.m. to 11:30 p.m., Saturday from 4 p.m. to 11:30 p.m., Sunday from 4 p.m. to 11 p.m. (404) 876-1111

SciTrek, 395 Piedmont Avenue. Open Monday through Saturday from 10 a.m. to 5 p.m., Sunday from noon to 5 p.m. Admission $7.50 for adults,

Stone Mountain Park

$5 for children ages 3 to 17, free for children under 3. (404) 522-5500

Silver Skillet, 200 14th Street N.W. Open weekdays from 6 a.m. to 8 p.m., Saturday from 7 a.m. to 1 p.m., Sunday from 8 a.m. to 2 p.m. (404) 874-1388

Southern Skillet, 1037 Alpharetta Street, Roswell. Open Monday through Friday from 6 a.m. to 9 p.m., Saturday from 6 a.m. to 3 p.m., Sunday from 8 a.m. to 3 p.m. (770) 993-7700

Six Flags Over Georgia, 7561 Six Flags Parkway S.W. (at I-20), Austell. Open daily during summer, weekends fall through spring. Admission $32 for adults, $21 for seniors and children ages 3 to 9. $5 parking. (770) 948-9290

Skate Escape, 1086 Piedmont Avenue. Open daily from 11 a.m. to 7 p.m., Saturday from 10 a.m. to 7 p.m. (404) 892-1292

Stone Mountain Memorial Park, Highway 78 East, Stone Mountain. Park open from 6 a.m. to midnight year round. Attractions open in the summer from 10 a.m. to 9 p.m., other seasons from 10 a.m. to 5 p.m. Park $6 per car. Admission to special attractions $3.50 for adults, $2.50 for children. (770) 498-5690

Three Dollar Café, 3002 Peachtree Road, Buckhead, (404) 266-8667; 8595 Roswell Road, Dunwoody, (770) 992-5011; 2166 Highpoint Road, Snellville, (770) 736-1000; 2580 Windy Hill Road, Marietta, (770) 850-0868.

Touch of India, 1037 Peachtree Street. Dinner from 5:30 p.m. to 10:30 p.m., lunch Monday through Saturday from 11:30 a.m. to 2:30 p.m. (404) 876-7777

Underground Atlanta, Peachtree and Alabama Streets. Store hours Monday through Saturday from 10 a.m. to 10 p.m., Sunday from 11 a.m. to 7 p.m. Admission free. (404) 523-2311

Varsity, 61 North Avenue N.W. Open Sunday through Thursday, 9 a.m. to 11:30 p.m., Friday and Saturday from 9 a.m. to 1:30 a.m. (404) 881-1706

White Water Park, 250 N. Cobb Parkway N.E., Marietta. Open summer from 10 a.m. to 8 p.m., Weekends in May from 10 a.m. to 6 p.m. Admission $20 for adults and children over 4 feet tall, $12 for children age 3 up to 4 feet tall, free for seniors over 62. (770) 424-9283

World of Coca-Cola, 55 Martin Luther King Jr. Drive. Open Monday through Saturday from 10 a.m. to 8:30 p.m., Sunday from noon to 5 p.m. Admission $6 for adults, $4 for seniors over 55, $3 for children ages 6 to 12, free for children under 6. (404) 676-5151

Wren's Nest, 1050 Ralph David Abernathy Boulevard S.W. Open Tuesday through Saturday from 10 a.m. to 4 p.m., Sunday from 1 p.m. to 4 p.m. Admission is $4 for adults, $2 for children ages 4 to 12. Storytelling $3 per person, all ages. (404) 753-7735

Yellow River Game Ranch, 4525 Highway 78, Lilburn. Open Monday through Sunday from 9:30 a.m. to 6 p.m. or until dusk in summer. Admission $5 for adults, $4 for children ages 3 to 11. (770) 972-6643

Zoo Atlanta, 800 Cherokee Avenue S.E. Summer hours open Monday through Friday from 9:30 a.m. to 4:30 p.m., Saturday and Sunday from 9:30 a.m. to 5:30 p.m. Winter hours daily from 10 a.m. to 4:30 p.m. Admission $9 for adults, $5.50 for children ages 3 to 11. (404) 624-5600

ANSWERS TO PUZZLES

page 7

page 13

page 17

page 19

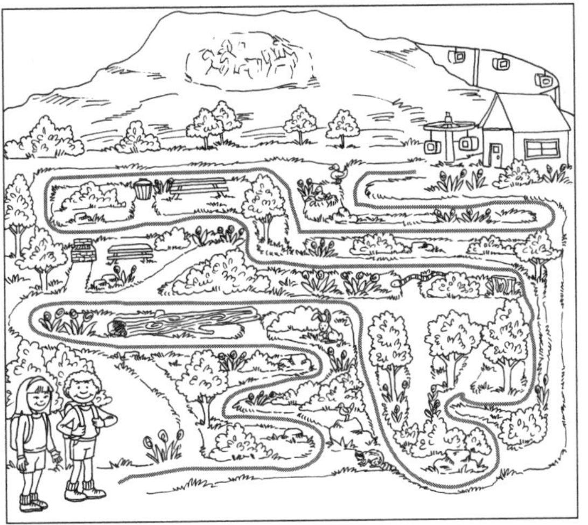

page 21

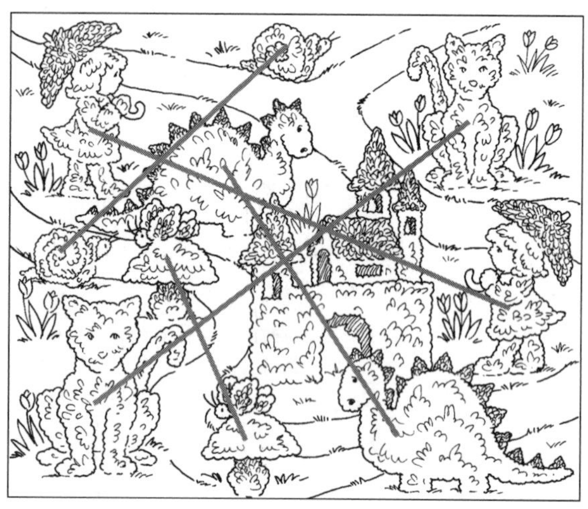

page 23

page 25

T R E E S K M E S O P M Y P V U H

H A L F K D Q R O S E S B I Y Q H

O R N B W H A P N D P V S W T C F

R T P V D A S K X T O N F S M U D

C I T T G S T L D M C D E S E R T

H E P A M D F E G N B R P T F S Y

I Q S A G U F N R T O U V E T W P

D A X S T C I N Y F C L W N A P W

S O T D U H R O N B A A A F M Q T

U A R E P Y S I L P F L O W E R S

R O X B L M A T E I P I L F N F W

D Y Q B I R D S Y R K S B E T Q R

page 27

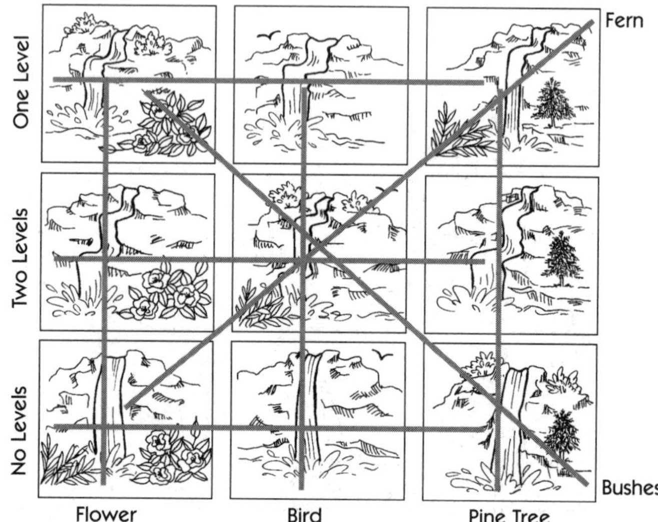

page 35

page 37

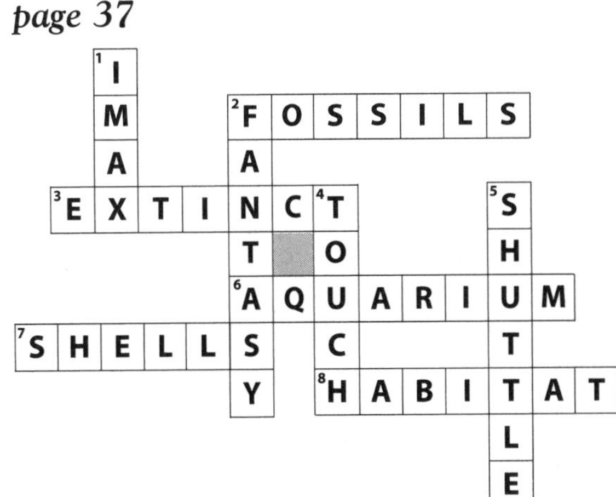

page 39

page 47

page 49

L F E B S L M E S A U D I E N C E

P I Y F V D Q S O X P L B D Y S H

O I G G A H L P E D P T Y W L T X

G T O H D Y W K X T O N T U E A D

F I R T T S N A D M I P N S I G N

H E C A M S F Y G A B O E T F E P

Y Q H I A U F N T T I U V E D W R

D A E T P C I R Y A C T R E S S O

S O S D U X U O M B O A G F E Q P

U A T E P C A R L P Y J N L R O S

C O R B L M A C O S T U M E S F W

D Y A B A R N Q Y R K S B E T Q R

page 59

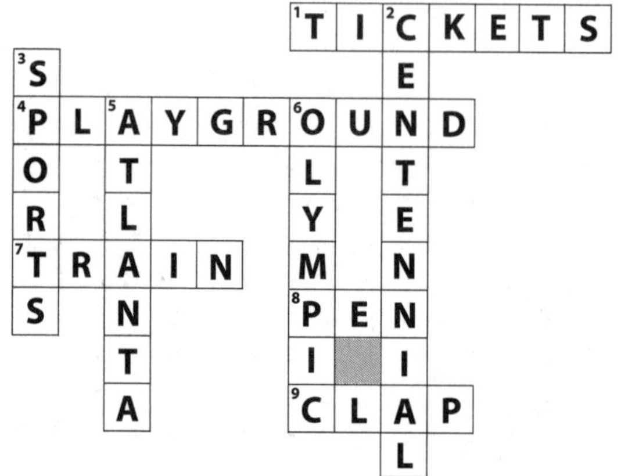

page 61

page 63

page 65

T F E B S L M E S T P M Y P V U H
P C Y F V D H E L M E T B B Y A H
O H N G T H L P N D P T S W A C X
G E P T D O W K X T E A M U E N D
F E Y A G S U A D M O P N S I V D
H R P C M U S C O R E B O A R D Y
Y L S K A U F N H T I U V E D W M
D E X L P C I N Y D C L W R A P A
S A T E U X L O M B O A G F A N S
U D R E P L A R L P Y W N L R O C
I E X B A M A T E I L O N F N F O
D R Q B A R N Q Y R K S B E T Q T

page 71

page 75

page 79

1 O	U	T	2 E	R	S	P	A	C	E	
			A							
3 S	T	A	R	S						
			T							
4 P	R	E	H	I	S	5 T	O	R	I	6 C
			Q			U				L
			U			R				E
	7 P	L	A	N	E	T				A
			K			L				R
			E			E				

page 83

page 89

page 91

page 95

page 97

page 103

page 105

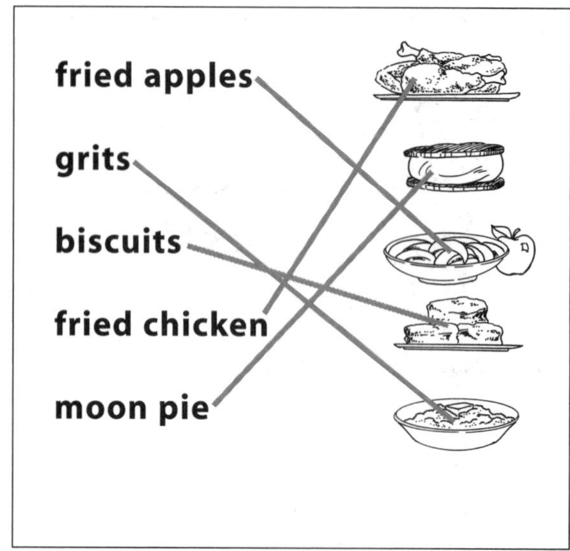

page 107

W B I S C U I T S T P M S P V U H
P A Y F V D Q J O X P B B D Y E H
O I C H I C K E N W I N G S L C X
G T P O D Y W K X R P A T U M L N
O G Y R G S I C E C R E A M O A N
H R P A M U F U G N B O E T O I Y
Y I S I L U C N H T R U V E N R P
P T X C H E E S E C A K E R P S W
I S T D B X R O M B O A G F I Q T
Z A R R P S A R L P Y J N L E O B
Z O A B L M A T E I L O M F N F W
A B Q B C O R N B R E A D E T Q R

page 109

page 111

page 113

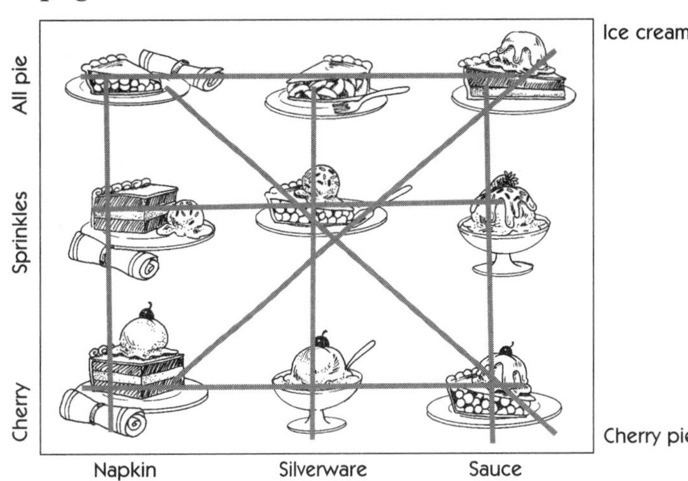

GEOGRAPHICAL INDEX: WHERE IS EVERYTHING?

INDEX

PHOTO CREDITS

Pages i, 56—Fran Conn; Pages ii—SciTrek; Pages iii (top), 68, 72 (both)—World of Coca Cola; Pages iii, 26 (both)—Amicalola Falls State Park; Page 1—Steven McGhee; Page 4, 8 (top), 20 (both), Page 38 (both), 76 (bottom)—The Write Idea; Page 5, 8 (bottom), 70 (both)—Atlanta History Center; Page 2, 6, 28 (both), 36 (bottom), 42, 44 (bottom), 48 (top), 50, 52, 54 (both), 74 (top), 80 (both), 82 (both), 84 (both), 90 (top), 94 (bottom), 96, 120, 122, 125—Georgia Division of Industry, Tourism & Travel; Page 10, 81 (both)—Jimmy Carter Library; Page 14, 18 (both), 86, 102 (bottom)—Georgia's Stone Mountain Park; Page 16 (both)—Lake Lanier Islands; Page 22—Kennesaw Mountain National Battlefield Park; Page 24 (both), 121—Atlanta Botanical Garden; Page 30, 32 (both)—ZOO Atlanta/J. Sebo; Page 34 (both)—Chattahoochee Nature Center, Inc.; Page 36 (top)—Fernbank Museum/Bernard J. Thoeny; Page 40—Yellow River Game Ranch; Page 44 (top)—© 1987 Alan McGee; Page 46 (top)—MARTA; Page 46 (bottom)—Westin Peachtree Plaza; Page 48 (bottom)—Fox Theatre; Page 58 (both), 60 (both), 92 (bottom)—Anna Brutzman; Page 62 (top)—Road Atlanta; Page 62 (bottom)—Atlanta Motor Speedway; Page 64 (both)—Georgia Dome; Page 66 (both)—Piedmont Park; Page 74 (bottom)—Center for Puppetry Arts; Page 76 (top)—Road to Tara Museum; Page 77—The Kobal Colletion; Page 78 (top)—Fernbank Museum of Natural History; Page 78 (bottom)—Fernbank Science Center; Page 88 (both), 90 (bottom)—White Water/American Adventures; Page 92 (top)—CNN Studio Tours; Page 94 (top)—Six Flags Over Georgia; Page 98—Cabbage Patch Kids; Page 100, 114—The Varsity; Page 102 (top)—Rib Ranch; Page 104—The Silver Skillet; Page 106 (top)—Rio Bravo Cantina; Page 108 (top)—Buckhead Diner; Page 108 (bottom), 124—Johnny Rockets; Page 110 (top)—Planet Hollywood; Page 110 (bottom)—Hard Rock Cafe; Page 112—The Cheesecake Factory.

Books for young readers ages 6 and up

from John Muir Publications

American Origins Series

Each is 48 pages and $12.95 hardcover.
Tracing Our English Roots
Tracing Our German Roots
Tracing Our Irish Roots
Tracing Our Italian Roots
Tracing Our Japanese Roots
Tracing Our Jewish Roots
Tracing Our Polish Roots

Bizarre & Beautiful Series

Each is 48 pages, $14.95 hardcover, $9.95 paperback.
Bizarre & Beautiful Ears
Bizarre & Beautiful Eyes
Bizarre & Beautiful Feelers
Bizarre & Beautiful Noses
Bizarre & Beautiful Tongues

Extremely Weird Series

Each is 32 pages and $5.95 paperback.
Extremely Weird Animal Defenses
Extremely Weird Animal Disguises
Extremely Weird Animal Hunters
Extremely Weird Bats
Extremely Weird Endangered Species
Extremely Weird Fishes
Extremely Weird Frogs
Extremely Weird Reptiles
Extremely Weird Spiders
Extremely Weird Birds
Extremely Weird Insects
Extremely Weird Mammals
Extremely Weird Micro Monsters
Extremely Weird Primates
Extremely Weird Sea Creatures
Extremely Weird Snakes

Kidding Around™ Travel Series

Each is 144 pages and $7.95 paperback.
Kidding Around Atlanta
Kidding Around Cleveland
Kids Go! Denver
Kidding Around Minneapolis/St. Paul
Kidding Around San Francisco
Kids Go! Seattle
Kidding Around Washington, D.C.

Kids Explore Series

Written by kids for kids, each is $9.95 paperback.
Kids Explore America's African American Heritage, 160 pages
Kids Explore America's Hispanic Heritage, 160 pages
Kids Explore America's Japanese American Heritage, 160 pages
Kids Explore America's Jewish Heritage, 160 pages
Kids Explore the Gifts of Children with Special Needs, 128 pages
Kids Explore the Heritage of Western Native Americans, 128 pages

Masters of Motion Series

Each is 48 pages and $6.95 paperback.
How to Drive an Indy Race Car
How to Fly a 747
How to Fly the Space Shuttle

Rainbow Warrior Artists Series

Each is 48 pages, $14.95 hardcover, $9.95 paperback.
Native Artists of Africa
Native Artists of Europe
Native Artists of North America

Rough and Ready Series

Each is 48 pages and $4.95 paperback.
Rough and Ready Homesteaders
Rough and Ready Cowboys
Rough and Ready Loggers
Rough and Ready Outlaws and Lawmen
Rough and Ready Prospectors
Rough and Ready Railroaders

X-ray Vision Series

Each is 48 pages and $6.95 paperback.
Looking Inside the Brain
Looking Inside Cartoon Animation
Looking Inside Caves and Caverns
Looking Inside Sports Aerodynamics
Looking Inside Sunken Treasure
Looking Inside Telescopes and the Night Sky

Other Children's Titles

Habitats: Where the Wild Things Live, 48 pages, $9.95

The Indian Way: Learning to Communicate with Mother Earth, 112 pages, $9.95

Ordering Information

Please check your local bookstore for our books, or call **1-800-888-7504** to order direct and to receive a complete catalog. A shipping charge will be added to your order total.

Send all inquiries to:
John Muir Publications
P.O. Box 613, Santa Fe, NM 87504